Solace in

By Amanda Bonnick
Poet in Residence—
Worcester Cathedral

love

Amanda Bonnick

Solace in the Silence

by Amanda Bonnick
Edited by Black Pear Press

First published in 2021 by Black Pear Press
www.blackpear.net

ISBN 978-1-913418-49-6

Cover photograph by Canon Stephen Edwards
Worcester Cathedral
Reproduced by permission of the Dean and Chapter
Of Worcester Cathedral

WORCESTER
CATHEDRAL

Black Pear Press

Foreword

It was a different era when Amanda first approached me to talk about the possibility of being our Poet in Residence. We made plans, we shared ideas, we delighted in possibilities—few of which we were to see fulfilled. Amanda was going to be inside the building, revelling in the space, allowing the place to speak to her as she turned thoughts into words. We were excited, enthusing each other over cups of tea.

The Cathedral Chapter was immensely grateful that, when the Cathedral was—along with every church—forced to close its doors in March 2020, Amanda's *Stations of the Cross* poems became part of our online offering. At the most significant point in the Christian year, when we were unable to meet for Holy Week and Easter, her words provided a real, daily, spiritual comfort for our growing Facebook community.

When I opened this collection, I expected poems. I was not prepared to find Amanda's journal of the year and the record, woven through in real time, of the emotions we experienced when the building was locked.

The poems about the Cathedral took on new meaning. No longer were these lines about the building, its beauty and inspiration, but lines about memory, and a yearning for comfort and security in uncertain times. There is a sense running through the collection of something very deep and precious—and a call to the reader to cherish and value the Cathedral and the faith that has built it. As the poems remind us, we may or may not be committed to the *church*, but many of us reach for that mysterious something when we need solace.

Poets have, down the ages, sought to frame the human experience and the elusive divine in their words. Amanda's collection continues this poetic vocation, locating us in a particular place and context, giving us a glimpse of something that transcends time and space, and allowing the building to speak out of the silence.
Canon Dr Georgina Byrne

Introduction

In June 2019 BC (Before Covid) I had been explaining to friends and family what the Poet in Residence role at the Cathedral would entail. I caught myself listing what I hoped to do and I suddenly got a frisson of fear, plus a hefty dose of humility. Uncomfortable. Who was I to try and encompass all that is the Cathedral? Those feelings, of being daunted by the self-imposed challenge, of being scared by the situations I would meet, of not personally being a good enough poet or person…well, I said to myself, those feelings must be acknowledged but not allowed to dominate. I gave myself a little lecture (I am prone to talking to myself. I have to check occasionally if it is out loud) and told myself it's right and proper to feel challenged when outside of your comfort zone but it must NOT (I got a bit bossy at this point) paralyse you or stop you from pursuing this exciting project. I was pretty sure most of it would be nothing like I planned it—some things will bomb; some will triumph unexpectedly, and I shall be changed by it. And the Cathedral will still be there, serene and strong and huge, at the end of it.

Well, I was right about one thing: most of it was *nothing* like I planned it. Who could have foreseen 2020 and a worldwide disease (I hesitate to say 'plague' for fear of sounding a little bit OT, never mind OTT) changing all our habits, our expectations, our lifestyles and, for too many, heralding extreme personal loss and tragedy.

Further back in April 2019, I was a bit giddy with the excitement of having just launched my first poetry publication, *Pick Your Own*, with the excellent and wonderfully supportive Black Pear Press. The launch was a great deal of fun and I was really encouraged by the response to the pamphlet. So much so, I began to put together the two things in my life that fascinate, obsess, haunt, fulfil me— writing, and the spiritual life.

I have always described myself as a pilgrim. I am curious about all aspects of the spiritual life, whether through the established main religions, or through intense individual responses and experiences. I think it is important. And, for me, the Cathedral is a place of solace and refuge and beauty, where I go to meditate and connect with all these things. I go there when relationships get complicated. I go there for Midnight Mass every Christmas Eve, where the story of a birth of an innocent child and all the hope and renewal it represents are present in the familiar, and beautiful, symbolism. I went there when my mother died and I just wanted solitude and comfort, along with the glory and inspiration of beautiful surroundings. It felt like being held.

It was a bit of a 'penny drop' then when I came up with the scheme to approach the Cathedral and put the proposition of having a Poet in Residence for a year. And that the poet should be me.

Fortunately, I approached exactly the right person. Canon Dr Georgina Byrne was a minister at the Cathedral and is also a published author. Perfect combination! She agreed to a meeting. I walked through the Cloisters, with local school artwork displayed and found I was unexpectedly nervous—I think because I was so very invested in this potential prospect. It meant a great deal to me and the thought of getting a polite 'No' was suddenly horrible.

But Georgina was lovely, and we discussed what we thought the potential residency would look like. Her enthusiasm was really encouraging. We agreed that it would track the liturgical year of the Cathedral and would include all the different communities that exist within it. It would include workshops led by me, open mic events, responses to the upcoming Three Choirs, Shakespeare in the Cathedral, Mayflower events. All this was exactly what I had hoped for! There was still the hurdle of the Chapter agreeing to this proposal, so I had to perform the mind-trick of simultaneously planning for all these exciting things, whilst also preparing for it not to happen. I managed this by realizing that I love the Cathedral and will write poems about it and follow the lovely organic flow of the Christian calendar anyway. Luckily the Chapter agreed, and a year and a half of extraordinary experiences was under way.

Contents

Foreword...iii

Introduction...iv

Contents vi

Worcester Cathedral 1

The Creed..6

How I'd Start a Church 8

Saturn's 62 Orbiting Moons 13

Darkness to Light...16

Untitled Poem 18

Christmas Crib Service 24th December 2019 19

The Size of Everything..20

Christmas Day 25th December 2019 23

Song School January 24th 2020...25

Crypt 27

Undercroft...32

Fifty Years Since Sarawak...34

Upper Vaults...36

Ropesight...38

Vergers...41

Manuscript 45

Introduction to Stations of the Cross Poems 49

Stations of the Cross 1 50

The Garden...50

Stations of the Cross 2 51

Betrayal...51

Stations of the Cross 3 53

Witness 53

Stations of the Cross 4 54

Peter..54

Stations of the Cross 5 55

Crisis Management..55

Stations of the Cross 6 57

Crown of Thorns 57

Stations of the Cross 7 59
A Quiet Day at Work 59
Stations of the Cross 8 61
In from the Country 61
Stations of the Cross 9 63
The Green Wood..63
Stations of the Cross 10 64
Perspective..64
Stations of the Cross 11 65
He Sees the Men 65
Stations of the Cross 12 67
Of All Women..67
Stations of the Cross 13 69
Untitled..69
Stations of the Cross 14 70
Until 70
First Catch..71
Introduction to the Women in the Gospels Poems 83
Oil and Tears 84
Woman Healed of a Haemorrhage 87
Feeding of the Five Thousand..89
Joanna..90
Jairus's Daughter..93
Pilate's Wife 94
Peter's Mother in Law 95
Woman Taken in Adultery 96
Mary Magdalene..98
The Healing 98
Mary Magdalene 100
Who do you say that I am?..100
Mary Magdalene 102
Who am I?..102
Mary Clopas..103
Mary Mother of Jesus I 105
Mary Mother of Jesus II 107

The Dangers of Art 107
'O, Woman.' 108
Salome I..110
Salome II...111
Woman of Samaria at the Well 112
Drawing Water from a Well.. 112
All the Other Women..113
Not Counting... 113
Annunciation 115
Lent 2021 116
Ministry..118
Thanks 120
Appendix...121
Debating Points...122
Reviews...123
Acknowledgements..126

Worcester Cathedral

Every day I take care to walk
on the other side of the street
to catch sight of my Cathedral
rearing up, misty-veiled,
sliding past as I walk on,
dominating the tumble
of tiny roofs, chimneys and aerials.
I know its every mood;
tinged and tinted by sunset,
charcoal under sombre skies,
golden lit against midnight.

Inside, hush fills the space.
Metaphor, symbol and meaning
live in stone, glass and fabric
and everything leads to the sunburst altar.
A child tries out the echoes.
Careful footsteps pick across intricately inlaid floors.

Small side chapels for private prayer,
privately uttered; Jesus Chapel,
St George's Chapel, Lady Chapel;
where hearts open to the still small voice.

Colour flows from stone to stone
as light changes through the day.
Rosy gold glows aloft,
cherubs picked out by soft shadows.
White marble mimics sleep,
and gold and brass glint
off crucifixes, candlesticks and monuments.
    In the Cathedral Cafe,
    just sitting,

I feel my worry sift
and sink.

My shoulders lighten
and the hat of headache,
worn all day, lifts,
as if in a polite gesture
to a lady.

13th June 2019. I am strangely reluctant to go into the Cathedral.
Now I have the green light on being resident poet I am feeling self-
conscious (ridiculous says my inner critic; who's actually watching?!)
I push through this feeling and go to sit in one of my favourite
places: the Lady Chapel behind the High Altar where there's an icon
of Mary holding a wriggling toddler who looks like he wants to
spring out of her arms, where the trees sway and flicker behind the
stained glass, sending moving shapes across the floor like living
flagstones of colour, where I notice Peter in the garden of
Gethsemane (why does he have a sword? Always wondered that),
where people light candles and send hope up to the glorious pink
and gold ceiling.

   Next a visit to Polly (Stretton) at Black Pear Press to discuss
possible book resulting from residency and she is completely on
board. So supportive! Always lovely to discuss poetry with her, over
a coffee and a biccie!

   I want to tell everyone but am waiting to meet the Cathedral
Operational Manager, Susan Macleod, to discuss a marketing and
publicity strategy, so don't want to step on anyone's toes. Difficult
to keep the news in though!

   I go into the Cathedral to get out of the heat. As soon as I walk
through the North Porch the blessed cool of centuries of thick
stone lowers my temperature and seems to unknot a few of the
stress ravels in my mind. Such a haven. It is big, so high, so wide,
like a huge embrace, it can encompass and hold anything. Any grief,

joy, resentment, anger, sadness, depression, can be brought here and held. And just that holding, that hug, helps the heart heal a little from whatever is troubling it.

1st July 2019. I receive an email to set up a planning meeting in September. It's getting real. It's not just in my head.

I start, over this summer, a complicated application for funding. Give up. Decide not to apply but to just write. I am not a funder. I hate forms. I am rubbish at selling myself. Therefore, I shall concentrate on the (rather large) job in hand. Phew, glad to get that self-imposed pressure off my chest.

I passed one of the tiny doors on South side of Cathedral today and glimpsed, briefly, the subterranean activity in the Undercroft. Workers everywhere, hard hats, dust. Exciting to imagine what the finished space will look like!

1st September 2019. Two weeks until first meeting and I have developed from nervous to frightened. I have a massive sense of humbleness. Who on earth am I to even try to represent this 1000-year-old building, repository of faith, beauty and sanctuary for centuries? I feel tiny, insignificant.

I remind myself—one step at a time. Break down the enormous challenge into small, manageable steps, practise mastery. Remember, you don't have to do all things brilliantly at once. It's a Learning Curve for me and for the Cathedral. As far as I am aware I am the first Poet in Residence, so there's no 'right way'. At the moment, there's only My Way!

Hope is in the altar, and in my heart.

One hour later, I planned a little, did some admin, diarizing, tidying, cleared the wilderness a bit. Feel a bit better.

The communities within the Cathedral I want to respond to: The Song School, The Education Department, the Vergers, The Ministers, The Library, the Stonemasons, the Congregation.

13ᵗʰ September 2019. Visit to Crypt after communion in Jesus Chapel: Reflection:

I get a bit contrarian, which is my wont. I like to be both inside the group and outside the group. This is a good thing for a poet, and especially a poet in residence, because one has empathy and insight into that which one is representing, but also the critical eye that the outsider viewpoint allows. It is not necessarily a comfortable position for a celebrant, however.

The homily is based on Mark 7 vs31-37 'ephphatha'—'be opened'. 'The string of his tongue was loosed and he spake plain.' This was one of Jesus' early miracles, enabling a dumb man to speak. This spoke to me (pun totally intended) about 'voices' and how we each have a voice and how this residency was going to challenge my own particular poetic voice and also challenge how I hear the different voices emanating from the Cathedral. How powerful it is that Jesus did this—the idea of letting someone be heard, enabling them to be fully understood, untying the tongue-tied, untangling the tangled, letting the arrow be loosed from the taut string of the tongue. A radical miracle. A risky miracle. People can be annoying with their varying views, different interpretations, disagreements. But Jesus let another note of potential discord be sounded. Yes, the healed man may well extol Jesus' miraculous powers now, but how many stood for Jesus after his arrest? Self-interest re-establishes itself pretty damn quickly. Not even Jesus' own beloved disciples or his cohort of devoted brothers stayed when the going got really tough. No doubt the dumb/deaf man might well be easily swayed/paid to speak against Jesus, call him a magician, an instrument of Satan, for the right price or just to avoid a beating. Remember all those who 'witnessed' against Jesus in front of the Sanhedrin, those who had been singing and lauding Jesus as he entered Jerusalem. Was this voice among them? But Jesus loosed his tongue, not knowing if he would sing like a bird, howl like a wolf or hiss like a serpent.

The homily went on to talk about vulnerability, opening ourselves up to be helped and healed. I certainly understood vulnerability, and how asking for help takes courage, is often the first step itself in self-awareness and healing. Who does not love Jesus the more when he begs God to let this cup pass him? When he doubts his own faith and ability to go on? I know I do. For me, that moment means more (well, at least as much) as the resurrection. Indeed, it *is* the resurrection, insofar as it is a mini death, a death of the ego, to ask for help, admit powerlessness, and be open to a higher power to heal through absolute love. It's the death of pride, the death of control, the death of a certain self-idea, identity. Those moments, those Gethsemane moments, when all around are asleep, heedless of your pain, and only you can acknowledge how everything is falling apart; those moments of the greatest darkness are the beginnings of the glimmers of dawn, of comfort, of a future. Ask, God is saying. Just ask. Drop the act of total control and acknowledge where you stand in this amazing creation. One drop in the ocean, but part of a magnificent wave cresting.

The Creed

Words made up by a warring Church
300 years after Jesus' death
(and non-apocalyptic appearance, I might add),
a meeting, a committee, a consensus, a taskforce,
a nice nibbling of pencils, a focus-group
to find the non-offensive, the meaningless,
the words we can all agree upon
which
nevertheless
NEVERTHELESS
NEVERTHELESS
sound glorious, make music,
in the ear and in the heart.
But they bypass the BRAIN,
which is also God-given.
and is a check on **nonsense.**
A check on think-tanks, corporate speak,
crap which keeps the non-existent peace,
until the next war.

All man-made organisations split and die anyway.
The Church's mistake is to think that it is not man-made.

And yet

A whisper sent on a warm breeze, a breath,
a promise, from centuries ago,
living, warm:
'Does no man condemn you?
then nor do I condemn you.'
'Truly, truly, I say to you,
today you shall be with me in paradise.'
'Tabitha cumi.'

The conclusion I draw,
my particular way of separating wheat from chaff?
Believe the words of love.
Ignore the words of power.

How I'd Start a Church

Start with the meal.
A Big Room. Circular.
A central hearth, an oven,
bread, warm, olive oil for those
who don't like their bread plain.

One person (different each time)
says the welcome,
splits the loaves,
sends them round the circle.
All chat, introduce each other, catch up.
A moment of thanks.
A reminder of love.

Then the wine.
Voices chatter more loudly.
Thanks given again.

Children play at the edges,
can join in when they understand,
when they want.

Then the one person (different each time)
asks for news, gives news,
asks for us all to hold those who suffer
in our hearts.
We might sing.
Let the songs be happy.
Dogs are allowed.
Cats sleep in puddles of sunshine.

We can stay if we want,
make plans to help each other,

ask for help ourselves,
be vulnerable, in the circle.
The circle of our arms.

18th September 2019. There is a meeting with Georgina and Susan Macleod to plan the Residency year. Georgina describes me as a gift and with that phrase, that generous choice of words, my sense of anxiety, pressure, self-imposed ridiculously high expectations, self-effacement…all slip from my shoulders. I feel that whatever I can offer will be enough, will be welcome, will be appreciated. It feels like an invitation to be part of something, albeit temporarily (but aren't we all temporary!) of a large, intricate, multifaceted community. What is apparent is that there are many communities within the single word 'Cathedral'; stonemasons, shop, Song School, café, vergers, ministers, admin, education, bellringers. And each one will be slightly differently organised and motivated. A challenge to describe and do justice to. I look forward to discovering each language, each vocabulary.

I feel empowered and energised!

So now it's official. I tell family and friends and then put out the news on Facebook (FB) I'm not yet on Twitter. The love and support and congratulations I receive feel wonderful. I remind myself, when I start to feel daunted by the magnitude, of Georgina's 'I am a gift' and that 'the Cathedral will be standing in 5 years, 10 years etc, completely unchanged by any of my scribbling, so let that be a freedom to you.' I don't have to conquer the building, or 'smash the brief'. I just have to add my own particular hand-chiselled brick to the monumental whole.

11th October 2019. A meditation, a story, a trance:

I am sitting in the Lady Chapel. Here a middle-aged woman is arranging flowers, getting rid of tired blooms, replacing them swiftly with a practiced, confident air. A toddler runs around, chirping some discovery to his parents. A couple contemplate the effigy of an 18th century woman who died of TB aged 42: 'So sad, so young,' they murmur.

I light a candle to my favourite icon, Mary, and a wriggling toddler Jesus. Thoughts of my own mother, and my children arise. I sit on a pew and close my eyes. I notice, in the soft darkness behind my eyelids, how noise retreats. How I feel alone with my tiredness, my stress, my thoughts, my prayer, even though I am surrounded by quite a few people visiting and enjoying the Cathedral. My heart rate slows. My thoughts become less busy and tangled. My shoulders drop and I sigh. Slowly the noises, conversations, tap of shoes on tiles, rustle of foliage, all fades. Soon I barely notice them.

Then I feel rather than hear someone sit down next to me. A movement of air, clothes falling into place, a warmth of a body close to mine. Too close. My serenity begins to dissipate, and I sigh again.

'Why do you sigh, sister?

I understand what the man is saying, even though it sounds strange. I open my eyes and turn my head to look. No one is there.

I am confused and look around. There had been warmth, and breathing and speaking. I do a full turn, but no one is near. I settle myself again. Close my eyes again. Try to relax.

'I am still with you, sister, by your side. Fear not.'

Again, the voice. It is rich, warm, and comforting. And next to me. I swear I can hear him breathe, feel his warmth. Noises from the Cathedral have ceased altogether. I keep my eyes closed this time. I want him to stay.

'Who are you?' I say, feeling foolish, worried I'll be thrown out for talking to myself, rambling like a madwoman.

My hand is covered by his on the seat. And his voice has a hint of laughter.

10

'You are not mad, sister. Do you not want to meet me? With all your heart and soul, your tears and prayers? Here I am. Be comforted.'

I say nothing. No need for words for he knows all that is in my heart. I soak up the warmth, comfort, love and security that emanate from him.

Eventually I say, 'I sighed because I wanted silence for my own thoughts, and everyone was being noisy.' So trivial, so petty, so selfish.

'You are hard on yourself, my dear sister. Silence is an infinite well inside you, fear not. Let the world wag on in its noise and strife, for you carry peace in your heart.'

I smile, eyes still closed.

A movement of air. An empty seat beside me. The sound of scissors clipping stems, a toddler laughing at peekaboo behind a pew. I open my eyes and no one is beside me. But I am not alone.

18th October 2019. So here is my first artistic decision of the residency. I am embarking (good travel metaphor) on what seems like a major enterprise. In order to be in time for Lent/Passion week (five months away), I have started work on writing fourteen poems in response to the Stations of the Cross. This means so much to me (almost as much as the whole residency ipse) that I want it to be the sombre magnificent jewel at the heart of the book. I may even think about publishing separately.

I am working hard at them; reading the Gospel verses, imagining myself in all their shoes, trying to find a unique through-line for each poem, investing a great deal of time in each one. This feels like the important work. At least for me. Where Jesus' humanity is so completely tested. There was a preliminary test, way back, three years before, in the desert, a bit like those trick questions at the job interview. He passed. But he had nothing to lose then. Here in Gethsemane, he has his life to lose, the ultimate test.

24th October 2019. On a personal note, my heart diagnosis has come through. I have a condition called aortic stenosis which will require surgery at some point. Good news is that it is not required for at least 10 years and I am fit and active in other ways and also, it has been picked up by my GP so now will be monitored and treated. So that can slot back into the background of my life and I can get on with enjoying the residency.

Stations of the Cross poems have got started. I have realised I can't do too much at any one time because it is harrowing and very sad. Imagine making the decision to set off on that journey, regretting it and then realising there is literally no getting off the roundabout. Your pain and misery are destined to go on and on until you die.

7th November 2019. Still working on Stations. 'It is finished' was the last one. It's difficult to find *my* particular poetic voice amidst all the hundreds of years of treatments in dry academic prose and rich poetry and lush paintings, of this scene.

1st December 2019. OFFFICIAL FIRST DAY OF RESIDENCY! It's the first day of Advent. I am in the middle of a craft project that has grown like Topsy. It started with a teensy suggestion by Susan to put some poetic excerpts on the Mayor's Christmas tree and now I'm cutting, sticking, prinking, folding, gluing, adjusting, ravelling, unravelling, dropping, ripping, all to put the Christmas gift labels on tables and all for a nanosecond of poetry per punter at the Mayor's Christmas Tea Party. And I am *not*, repeat not, a craftswoman, so God knows what they will look like.

Saturn's 62 Orbiting Moons

(St Richard's Hospice Light Service November 2019)
November gloom fills the space.
Tiny lights push
the edges of night.

Hands hold small candles
ruffed with cardboard
like Saturn's rings.

Our longing could run a million power stations,
light a trillion bulbs,
to shine into indifferent space.

Out there, a speck of dust
travels a distance
from the planet Saturn.

It has gravity, existence, presence
and so helps create, through its constancy,
the majestic rings of Saturn.

Gravity forms the order of the rings.
Sixty-two moons sweep through,
affecting their course.

Thousands of bands,
within the influence of the moons,
dust and debris glinting,

shimmer in our sun's discarded light.
At eighty thousand kilometres an hour
their shards sparkle.
In the same way

all the molecules of our universe
come into being
at their particular time,
particular gravity,
particular co-ordinates,
and create astonishing symmetry
and ineffable beauty.

And it is our honour now
to see this universal truth in the lives we mourn;
their particular trajectories,
particular love,
their particular lifetimes,
and their ineffable beauty.

Advent Procession Candles, wax drops, drips, hands holding, handheld, gloved hands, loved ones, light glowing, shining, dark receding, carols proceeding, voices soaring, glory in the highest where the motes of dust float to the top of the ancient oaks that hold up the ark of light floating in a darkened world, ancient voices join our weak and unused tongues, to swell the congregation well above its normal 2000. If we listen, we can hear the robin and the sparrow join the choir, a higher hymn from nature, creatures all in this waiting time of hibernation. Warm, deep rich shadows stretch up, mid-arch a shelf of candles stretches around the Cathedral, spans its midriff. I add and add; there must be over 200 thick candles glowing through the darkness.

My first 'gig' as resident poet—a full Cathedral, darkness fills its huge cradle, slim tapered candle in cardboard holder. Light moves from person to person, glowing up into faces. A small warmth accompanies each single flame. The service is one and a half hours long but passes swiftly. I am engaged with each piece of music, each reading. It is a theme of prophecy about to be fulfilled, of waiting, of hope, of expectation, of the seed of anticipation planted in the deep black earth of winter. Then we wait for the green shoot, for the return of the sun. A time to sit, suspended, pregnant, trusting in the faith that what is to come will come in its own good time. The sermon is on 'doors' vs 'doorways'. Doors exclude, shut out whereas doorways invite, include, promise, tempt, wait. Isaiah 22 vs22 'I will place on his shoulder the key of the house of David. Key of David—he shall open, and no one shall shut; he shall shut and no one shall open.' Isaiah 28 vs16 'A precious cornerstone, a sure foundation.'

So, for me, a start, a beginning, an excitement, a fear, a thrill, a challenge.

Advent Cathedral December 1ˢᵗ 2019

Darkness to Light

We hold onto this glowing thread
when all about is cold darkness.
A seed planted long ago
in the black earth of winter.
We wait, then, and trust.

Carols proceed; voices soaring glory
to the top of the ancient oaks
shoring up this light-filled ark,
floating in a darkened world.

We are joined by centuries of voices
to swell the congregation.
Let's listen hard to hear, also,
the robins and the sparrows
on a twilight College Green,
unseen through dusk,
but carolling to drive out shadows,
bring in hope.

Dark recedes, waxy drops drip.
Hands hold loved ones, lost ones.
Light catches, spreads through deep rich shadows,
a shining circle of warmth and waiting.

I now have a lanyard that says 'Poet in Residence' under the
Cathedral logo. So proud! That photo goes on FB!
    Remember those Christmas poetic gift labels that I created in a
Blue Peter manner? I created over 30, spending three evenings
surrounded by printouts, glitter, ribbon and robins. Now I hear the
Mayor's Tea is cancelled. All because a measly General Election has

been called on that day. How very inconvenient and selfish.

So, after the disappointment, and the panic attack when I couldn't find the poems I'd been working on, I start having glimmers of how I want the work to pan out. I know I am going to do a series of poems on the Stations and as a counterbalance I want a similar number of poems of the women in the Gospels. The named women, the unnamed women, the invisible, inaudible women who were nevertheless there, and the big players. This feels, trying hard not to be over the top, like the sacred work. I am very much risking sounding pretentious, but when I write a poem from a person's point of view, I get myself into a position of opening up to hear their voice, of an imaginative leap into their position (as far as that is possible at all). A sort of trance. I read as much as I can, I imagine their world from all the senses, I try to place myself in their day, their needs, their dreams, their boundaries. I try to see what they see. My fears are that my resultant poems do not reach these high ambitions.

Political Opinion Alert!
December 13th (A Friday, how apposite) 2019. A sombre day— complete landslide for the Tories and their 'Get Brexit Done'. Apparently, that was the only issue. Argh.

I am in the Cathedral. I have come here for escape, perspective and balm for my very troubled spirit. I have wandered in the cloisters and looked at all the Christmas trees there. Each one is a labour of love and creativity plus a call for help for one good cause or another. They are dazzling, twinkling, subtle, garish, beautiful, quirky reminders that most people are mostly good and well-meaning.

For me the prospect of five more years of Tory neglect and pseudo-austerity is heart breaking. It feels devastating. It feels important. It feels dangerous (1930s anyone?). So, this building provides me with perspective. Not only does it get me out of my small house, it gets me out of my small mind. I see large, hushed, humming spaces, with colour and beauty everywhere. I see folk being purposeful, carrying on. And I remember that this building has sat here for over 1000 years. It has seen wars, bloody rebellions, civil strife, poverty, huge social changes. It has withstood bombardment from the Nazi skies. It remains, tranquil, always full of hope, always representing a better way of doing things; love thy neighbour, do good unto those who persecute you, forgive seventy times seven, turn the other cheek. For what else is there? Only the perpetuation of fear and anger. We can all halt that slide to the bottom, by being our own loving selves.

Untitled Poem

Sore at heart
on my knees
I come to the place
that understands.

Here an embrace
of centuries old walls,
here surrounded
by soothing calm.

Heartbeats slow,
panic stills.
I look up and
Mary is there, holding her baby,
as always.

Christmas Crib Service 24th December 2019

Packed to the rafters,
every seat taken, every pew,
coats marking places,
families spilling up and down altar steps,
excited children running.

A constant, heaving mass
of 'where's my drink/hanky/snack?'
Stolid, solid donkey,
mildly interested.
Hymns sung too high
and I am breathless, hoarse,
wanting so much to sing like a bird.

Children chase animals,
upstaging grown-ups.
Microphones echo and distort,
words are lost.
Lucky we all know this story.

And here we are, in a Cathedral
feeling like a theatre, like a farm,
a city, a night, a medieval meeting place,
a pub, a stable, a crib, an embrace.

The Size of Everything

'Her body will do what it must.'

Kind words from the woman of the house,
her arm around my waist
throughout my slow descent
from the tired donkey.
She helps me limp-footed into the back room,
to a soft bed of straw.

'But will she need food, for strength?'
He means well, but the thought sickens me.

'Dear Heavens above! Men!'
A shove and he is sent next door
for water and a little wine.
'Perhaps a crust of bread to gnaw on.'
She saves his face.

Then, blessed silence.
Thick darkness falls around us.
A small oil lamp flickers shadows
onto the beaten earth and up the rock walls.
A shift, a sigh, an animal warmth.

'Soon be here, lovey; your belly's hardening.'

Something is taking over my body.
This body that has danced
through olive groves
to the lake's shore,
swum beyond any man's gaze,
young and strong through the water.
Now it is tightening, tightening, tightening,

winding up deep within me.
And something cracks.
I cry out,
and flood all over the dusty floor.

She lays me on my side,
pulls up my legs,
strokes my forehead.
'That's normal, lovey.
It's happened to every woman and now it's your turn.'
She laughs,
'It's what happens when you let love in.'

I let love in and now it's fighting to get out.
But love is huge, the size of the strange star,
the size of the blown indigo sky,
the size of everything,
And it hurts.

'That's it, let it come, and when it does,
bloody well push!'
We are both sweating now.
My cries fill the cave.
I bloody well push.

Three shadows on the wall,
starlight creeping through the shattered door,
a cow lowing softly.

Then I am beached,
high above the tideline
and the pain has gone.
Love is in the room.
She kneels between my legs, grinning.
'A boy, dear one. A sweetheart, a boy.'

She places him in my arms,
helps me sit, covers my legs,
and wipes my face, bidding me drink.
And through all her care, I look on him.

Dark eyes, universes, swallowing me,
wet hair, a crumpled face.
He turns his cheek to my breast
and a sharp pain starts
near my heart.

My body aches and is sore
but I don't ever want to move from here.

The woman sighs.

'Will you see them now, lovey? Your visitors?'

The old door opens and new faces peer in.
I am astonished; the whole world has come
to lay its treasures at his feet.

'Can I come in too?'
Amused, shy, he enters, to see his son.

The woman leaves, the visitors withdraw
and we gaze on our son
who, though he sleeps,
holds all our hearts in his hands.

Christmas Day 25th December 2019

A new baby wakes, fresh,
eyes moving from face to face,
hope to hope, meeting only love.

Once black slaves
chanted their spirituals of pain
and Match Girls laid down their meagre tools
to protest their sordid lives.
Two hundred years ago, tiny children
dodged and weaved between speeding looms,
sucking cotton dust into perfect lungs

Throw back the curtains,
cheeks blushing at the first touch of cold
and see the new day.
Each day is Christmas day when we awaken;
see the Christ child on your nativity shelf,
see him in the yellow dinghy bobbing,
in the high, cold waves of the Channel,
see him caged in the Deep South heat,
see him crying, covered in dust
in the back of an ambulance.
See him in your neighbour's quiet child.
And see him in your torn and precious self.

January 3rd 2020. A new start. I'm on the other side of Christmas. I am trying and failing to combat overwhelming feelings of ennui and exhaustion. However, I have my poetry and the new year of Cathedral engagement to look forward to. I have contacted the vergers, the bellringers, the Song School, the undercroft/education department and am enthused to meet them all and start writing about them.

January 24th 2020. And now my first engagement of the year at the Cathedral—a visit as an observer to the Song School. I meet all the Year 7s and 8s in the little kitchen beforehand, where they are having bagels, toast and drinks after school, before the practice. I chat with them for a bit—they are very self-possessed, well mannered and chatty. Then Mr Hudson appears and calm order is established. Obedient boys (plus an obedient poet) follow the imposing figure upstairs to the rehearsal room. The rest is in the poem. Suffice to say I was very grateful for the experience and the insight and the fun!

Song School January 24th 2020

The sun slowly leaves the sky,
winter trees scratch bruised clouds.
The smell of toast and bagels
rises in the warm kitchen.
Boys eat, chat, rock back and forth
on chairs, as all boys do.

The Music Master arrives
and we are off to a bright white room,
high desks, stools and a piano, central.
Straight into it,
their voices bounce off walls
and blast me back into my place.
Where do they pack the air in their tiny frames?
They should be round as red balloons,
tethered and bobbing.

'All eyes on me,' bringing the boys back,
phrase by phrase, breath by breath, to focus.
'Be together in the silence
and the singing will take care of itself.'
The fall and glide of the reassuring hand
showing not only the beat,
but the feeling.

The rehearsal is grooving;
technique and emotions marry in a wall of sound.
My eyes close, and all is song.

Full dark outside;
black windows mirror
a little room of light sailing,
ark-like, on an ocean of sound,

a sea of midwinter might.

The trebles rise above deeper resonance.
Music fills the room, flows
out the open doors and down
the stairs and we follow,
through the house,
the secret Song School door,
and into the Cathedral cloisters.

Now it is Evensong.
I take my seat and they enter, altered.
The service starts as it does every evening;
the holy words not the only solace for hurt hearts
and lost souls, but also the clear young voices
singing ancient wisdom,
breath and voice and feeling and focus
all together, praising God.

Sunday 2nd Feb 2019. I have heard from Georgina that my Stations of the Cross poems will be framed and put up around the Cathedral nave on the pillars. I am so excited by this! So now I am in Boston Tea Party (my main place of work when I am writing, either poetry or fiction—gets me out of the house and its distractions) and I am looking at the 13th Station of the Cross. The one where Jesus dies. And I cannot write it. I cannot approach that mystery, encapsulate that event, that event that resounds through millennia, through universes. There have been so many depictions in art, prose and poetry—heartbreakingly beautiful and eloquent. Who am I to add to these? Perhaps I need a caveat at the top of each poem: 'I am not worthy'. This poem will take a long time to write. Be still. Let it speak.

Monday 3rd Feb 2019. I just had echocardiogram at hospital (where, after much painful pushing and shoving the device showed up a tiny, calcified, game, brave, persistent pulsing aortic valve.) I felt quite moved that it had kept me alive thus far. Moved and grateful.

I go to the Cathedral.

I sit, looking at the Mary and Jesus icon, with the tender, slightly exasperated look on the mother's face. I let the solid, soft silence descend on me, quiet my busy mind. I close my eyes, almost near to sleep, but not quite—a sort of hovering between my consciousness and that of others. A slight withdrawal of self from others. This place does what it always does: soothes and heals.

I feel the Cathedral breathe. I think of my heart and the red and blue blood, oxygenated and non-oxygenated and I marvel at the mechanisms and processes inside me, keeping me alive. A poem comes.

Crypt

Can you hear the Cathedral breathing?
Listen until you are dizzy.

Close to its heart
where the exchange takes place,
draw in your breath in pain,
exhale in absolution and love.
Here, where dark and light
flicker at each other's edges.
Where death meets life
and the deep blue
turns a rich red.
This is the sacred engine room
where enlightenment
turns,
like a fish in deep waters,
felt but not seen.

The breath, the word,
the pneuma, the spirit,
all are one
and all are held here.

Tuesday 4ᵗʰ Feb 2020. I sit in the Jesus chapel, open for prayer,
and try to pray for someone who has just killed himself. But I am
closed for prayer.

Black and white
the marble tiles stretch out.
So binary.
Yes. No.
Black. White.
On. Off.
Alive. Dead.

We are never 'half-dead'
or 'half alive'.
We say these phrases
but they both mean 'alive'.
We are, until we are not.

I try to pray.
The tiles seem to move
beneath my searching gaze.
Shift and perplex
but still black and white.
He had a wife he loved.
He had children he loved.
He was popular
and made people laugh.
Where then did his anguish reside?

We keep our wounds hidden
our grief unpresented.
The sun shines gaily
off our polished armour.
'We must have a coffee' I'd said.
I wish I'd fixed a date.

Wednesday 5th February 2020. It's my birthday—hurray! I'm 58—
~@*%!

What has cheered me up—meal at Café Rouge last night,
presents from my family and friends and a lovely brekkie this
morning.

Plus…an extremely interesting and inspiring tour of the nearly
finished Undercroft at the Cathedral. I feel very honoured and
excited and have notebook, pen and questions at the ready! Hi Vis
jacket, hard hat and tough boots, H&S regs and signing off, past
barriers the public may not pass (boosting my sense of self-
importance, which my birthday cards kicked off this morning!) The
Site office is on a building site within piles of plastic pillows of
aggregate, sand, lime products, recycled bricks from 19th century
(kept 'just in case'. I learn this is what conservators do) now coming
into their own. Stone cutting machines, face masks for dust. And
what dust…on everything. Snowdrops and crocuses spread out
under enormous trees nearby. The sky is bright blue and the day is
crisp. I am very happy.

We enter just below the Song School—old stone steps have
gone (stone kept, just in case) to be replaced. Old glass is re-used to
create new panel between the Undercroft and King's Hall. A
mediaeval arch was unknown until recently uncovered, its arch a
semicircle sunburst of edges of slate. A cheeky stone head peeks
out, re-attached now to where it belongs.

The low roof wheels over our heads, spreading out like tree
branches from 4ft diameter trunk pillars. A man picks away at
emulsion; a long and tedious job, done with care and attention. No

29

Radio 1 blaring away, no disrespectful banter. Just the chip of chisel and mallet. The floor is nearly there, another layer to add of Forest Green sandstone tiles, to cover heating, pipes, electricity.

A stonemason, as we watch, is forming a window from inside, so the metal grid goes outside and cannot harm the stonework. Every new stone is matched to old stone beneath. The 14th century method of hot lime mortar is used. If a mediaeval stonemason turned up now, in woollen top and trousers, leather apron and belt, he would not look amiss among these workmen and women. They speak the same language, touch, and they understand the same stone, mortar, wood and metal. The same processes are at work to form the same utility and beauty. The walls are blackened by decades as it has been used as a coal store. Soot etches everything.

A shaft of light shows the way, directs our gaze to where the window will be. The architect explains how modern plasters are stitched amongst the old: We need to show where we are, to be honest about our repairs (we're not pretending to be old) but also to take our place proudly in this tapestry of ages and artistry. Patchwork of centuries that play together and create a living, used building. She continues: what we always come across—bats and asbestos. Asbestos is cleared away safely, walls washed and then sealed (encapsulated) so H&S rules are followed.

We can ask questions. The stonemason replies—we are more than builders, we conserve, it is in our blood; my father, grandfather and great grandfather tended the lime pits—it's my legacy and my responsibility to our country's architectural heritage. He touches the wall where a thousand years ago a man, with skills such as his, also touched, used his senses and his wits to shape the stone that holds the sacred space.

Then we get to see Christ in Majesty, in the old refectory of King's School. Research about this enormous stone relief depiction of Christ reigning in glory after his resurrection is still needed and is ongoing. Theories are manifold and slippery. Destroyed in parts (Christ's face, the angels) by Henry VIII's destructive power, it is thought possibly finished off by Edward VI. Some say it is the largest Christ in Majesty in Europe. It had been completely plastered over until 1890 when a violinist, perhaps over-bowing, poked a sharp elbow into the plaster and a large chunk fell off, revealing the stonework below.

It is currently unstable (I know how it feels) and needs lime mortar repairs to keep it safe. It will not be restored, just made safe. One idea is to project over it so one can see what it may have looked like.

Final part of our tour—archaeology. A trench dug for drainage and pipeage for toilets for the renovated Undercroft has yielded some finds which need investigation and expert analysis. Archaeologist is being a bit cagey—would not come down one way or another as to what has been found. It will be closed up for good after the dig and tarmacked over. We await the results of their finds.

Undercroft

The low roof vaults over our heads,
branching from rooted trunks of pillars;
an unknown arch rays outwards, a sunburst of slate,
cheeky stone head peeking round its edge.
My gaze follows a shaft of sunlight up to a tiny window
where one man, hard hat, hi-vis, laddered, works.
Chip, chip, chip of chisel and mallet.

'We are more than builders; we conserve.
It's in our blood—my father, grandfather, great-grandfather,
all worked like this.' He gestures to the tools,
the stone, the buckets of mortar.

Chip, chip, chip of chisel and mallet.
Ten centuries ago and the stonemason,
in woollen cap and leather belt
takes his place, works the stone, dust rising,
trowels the hot lime mortar.
He matches and patches each new stone
to the old beneath, stitching
his present to his past, talking
in hope to us, his imagined future.
And we, here, excited about *our* future,
tip our hats to him and share this:
a heritage that shapes the stones
that hold this sacred space.

Susan has emailed about BBC H&W wanting to do an interview re the residency. Hurrah! press attention.

14th February 2020. This anniversary, rather than being a reminder of cupid's arrow, has a sadder meaning for me. It is 57 years since my father died, 14th February 1963. I was only one year old. He was a Squadron Leader in the RAF and died in a plane accident in Borneo. We were stationed in Singapore and all had to leave immediately—going from tropical heat to the coldest winter thus far (1963), and all whilst in shock and grieving. I would light all the candles in the Cathedral if it could enable me to see him. No metaphor, no hidden insight, just pure love and longing.

14th February 2020. St George's Chapel, Worcester Cathedral

Fifty Years Since Sarawak

The flags of battles long ago
flutter gently in the warming draft,
and faded fringes ripple
as if recalling an ancient fray.
Horizontal, they fill
the silent, cold, stone chapel

I am here to mark a certain turn of years,
memorialise my father and find
a gentle solace in the moment.
A rush of thoughts but tears won't come.
The hum of heaters underpins the hush
and elsewhere voices echo, indistinct.

Blue Spring sky shines through jewelled glass.
I blink and the jigsaw assembles into
a young St George, golden and protective,
behind each soldier, sailor, airman.

So where were you then, when my father's plane
fell from a different sky, a different time,
into that hot green jungle, far away?
Not between him and his violent death.

No.

Just as these small words do not stand
between me and a daughter's grief.

Yesterday I went to the Cathedral to meet Georgina and reporter from BBC to record an interview. It went well and was fairly straightforward. However, I completely forgot to include a poem to read (I am not one of those poets who memorise their own poems) so I had nothing. A lesson for the next time!

So, I also today have what I am calling a 'Verger Afternoon'. I am in time to have a personal and impromptu tour of the Upper Vaults. Dear Reader, it is now I must tell you that I suffer from a visceral and whole-body fear of heights and there is no will-power on earth that can shake that, so that is the context for this tour…I have to summon all my courage, steel my sinews and also bring to bear my natural disinclination to look like an idiot, in order to actually do the tour without passing out. I manage and I think no one notices.

I meet Nathaniel, a young, very helpful and kind verger, and also a tour guide (whose name escapes me—sorry!) who is brushing up his spiel and needs someone to test it on. We start by going into one of myriad little old wooden doors that lead to exciting and secret places that abound in the Cathedral. I knew where we were when we started—I oriented myself—but by the time we climb 100 steps twisting up to the left all the time, I have no idea. A crouch through a tiny door, a hop up an over-high step and then along a disturbingly slim corridor (2ft wide and only just higher than me). We then walk out onto a walkway which is the spine of the vaulted ceiling you can see from below. It is rough-hewn, plastered roughly and each crevice is filled with bits and bobs of stone and plaster. The wooden beams arc over all, with some many centuries old. This is awe-inspiring enough and the guide is knowledgeable and entertaining about its history. But we've only just started.

Upper Vaults

Through tiny, strange-shaped doors,
onto staircases
spiralling up, tighter and tighter,
then a long drop,
above arched and vaulted ceilings
turned inside out, a beached whale,
onto the rough-plastered spine of the beast.

We crouch through another low door,
hop up a high step, turn twice,
like blind man's bluff at height,
and we're in the Barbers' room,
where monks used to rest;
this aerial living space secretly soars
above the beauty of the Cathedral.

Higher still, we feel the murmuring presence
of the 16 bells, trembling in the tower.
Then we exit, widdershins, twisting
down the corkscrew stairs
until we are debouched
into the glory of the nave.

How we ended up on the other side of the aisle
I do not know. I cannot rule out magic.

Off now to the Barbers' room, monks' rest room which in previous centuries would have been connected to all the rooms above the body of the Cathedral, creating an aerial living space unbeknownst to the congregation far below. En route we glimpsed down into the nave and towards the West Window. That particular moment was dizzying and stomach-clenching. My problem is not mainly my fear of falling (though there is that) but a fear of jumping. I just get such an urge to leap out into space and then I scare myself silly.

Then we reach the bell tower by another secret, almost magic door. What an impressive room—bells hang in the 1869 oak frame which is known locally as the Wigwam. The bells, in all their mighty weight and gravitas press down from above. I can't see them (all 13) but can feel their presence, almost hear a faint thrumming as if a gentle toe-tap could set the bells off, a-trembling, touching each other gently, talking their own language of tongues and clappers.

Ropesight

The hand is there before the conscious thought.
The sally fits the palm before the pull,
the pull before the headstock turns
on gudgeon pins, and the bell,
all nearly five hundred kilogrammes,
begins its massive swing,
before the clapper meets the lip
of the ever-smiling mouth
and sounds the first chime of the peal.

Ropesight, it's called.

Worcester trains its ringers well,
like high tower, belfry-living pilots,
who simulate through software
the carillon, the peal,
until the practice is held deep
in the bones, the marrow, the muscle,
and the cry, 'Catch hold!' calls
all instincts into play,
and they feel the rope on skin,
sending the collective intent
to the mighty giants sleeping in the belltower.

Visit six brass-tongued beauties, grandees now,
cloistered in genteel retirement,
recalling past peals.
Examine them from their crown,
past their waist, that tender indent of a shapely sway,
to their open mouths, stoppered
on the stone resting place.
A regular epitaph is engraved on each.
They hold, like Oak or Redwood,

in their dendrochronology,
the history of these small islands:
peals for this coronation,
muffled belling for that stately death,
and the joyous clamour of the quick ding dong
for celebration and relief at the end of war.
Each event marked and rung.

And when the nation mourns,
Worcester, alone of all churches,
rings with the harmonic minor, the lament,
the haunting, plaintive sound
that accompanies each New Year's Eve,
Remembrance Sunday and Good Friday.

And when the nation fears and invasion threatens
the bells fall silent.
A cold, frightening time
when normal rhythms are stilled
and we tiptoe through our days, waiting.

Then we make our way back down. Thighs are now properly
aching. I meet Robert, another Verger, in the Vergers' room, which
used to be a punishment room for naughty monks, with a small
window so they could still participate in mass. There are venerable
old faces peering out from oil paintings, one of whom is Woodbine
Willie. In this portrait he is looking rather lugubrious which, from
photos I have seen, is not his normal expression. Here Robert and
the Tour Guide have a learned debate about how Oswald was not
from Cluny but Fleury (or vice versa). Then Nathaniel and I meet
Carol who is dusting and polishing the intricate, carved misericords
with beeswax spray. The smell is as exotic and pungent as any
incense.
    As we speak, I look around the Cathedral, taking in its size and

the complexity (to say the least) of its 'fixtures and fittings' and I marvel at how these dedicated Vergers—four of them—keep it immaculate and beautiful, alongside all their other duties. I learn about hints on how to get red wine from white linen (a constant hazard), how to dust the very top of the rood screen (wait for scaffolding and then grab your chance up there amongst the workmen). I learn they are open 7 days a week, 52 weeks of the year from 7am 'til 6pm, unless there is an event on in the Cathedral, which there often is. I learn that all Vergers are First Aid trained, connected by smartphone to each other and the other departments, act as Front of House (FOH), advisors, security guards, a gentle tactful presence in the nave, impromptu tour guide, napery preparers, silver polishers, chair (100s of them) movers and that they lead processions in church services, and are backstage crew to visiting events. They are the public face of the building, are people who love and care for the space and who serve those who use it. Their dedication and love shine bright as the gleam on the ancient oak, the glint of the sun through the stained glass, the tremor of light on the chalice. If you ever need someone to help in the Cathedral, a person in a long dark red robe, or magenta fleece, will cheerfully aid you. Unsung. But I sing them now.

Vergers

From the Vergers' own rest room
portraited by austere gentlemen,
where we take a breather,
I follow to the misericords,
where she is busy polishing
(Sisyphean task) the intricate carvings,
with incense-smelling beeswax.
Generous with her anecdotes,
photos, insights, history,
she sings her duties
with a loving and faithful tongue;
First Aid, Security, Open up,
Close up, Type up
Health and Safety protocols,
Scene Shifter, Procession Leader,
Red Wine Remover, Launderer of Linen,
Source of Arcana, etc.
More etcetera, in fact, than you could shake a duster at.

Above all, perhaps, they are silent comfort-givers;
circulating discreetly, in blood-red sweatshirts,
everywhere,
as they dust, clean, sort and tidy;
for those who arrive at the Cathedral to sit
in distress or loneliness.
It's like going to sleep at night, fearing a nightmare,
a monster under the bed,
a shadow by the wardrobe,
and hearing your mother washing up downstairs.

The backdrop to the next sequence is the floods we Worcester folk come to expect this time of year.

Wed 19th February 2020. I am building up these workshops on Friday into something to dread. I've prepared (over-prepared?), got resources, copies and I am just stewing in anxious thoughts now imagining the worst. I know once it is up and running that I'll be fine, more than fine, I'll enjoy it. But the pre-performance nerves are no fun at all.

So, I go to my poems for solace. Playing with words, moving them around like scrabble tiles, until they make some sense and sound right.

Sunday 23rd February 2020. Well, the workshops happened. The first had 0 attendees (perhaps hard to get to Cathedral through floods?) I had a long chat with the two volunteers assigned to help me. Then I consoled myself with cake and tea (at the Education Department's expense) and then had a massive cheese and pickle sandwich (on mine). Then I waited for the second workshop at 2pm. I had persuaded myself that it too was going to be a no-show, a disaster, but in the end 6 children and their very supportive parents turned up. Isobel, Isla, Olivia, George, Matthew and William. All entered into the spirit of it and produced a lot of words and a lot of ideas. Takeaways for me: 1. Read a poem or two at beginning to exemplify and inspire. 2. Give much more time to the actual writing!!

Olivia's story: Werewolves escaping persecution on earth via space rocket, requiring virtual reality screens to block out the view of the moon (in case they transformed)

Isobel's story: She wanted to write a series of 12 novels about a shy but adventurous girl called 'Annabel' and wanted to be the youngest published author. I hope she is still working towards that goal.

William's story: A Viking story which started, 'Here I am, at the docks, surrounded by…' what an impressive opening line! Straight

42

into the action.

Matthew: Wrote a fabulous rhyming poem about the use of Lego bricks to record events. What a great idea!

George was enamoured of his quill pen and flourished it mightily.

I got a lovely hug from Isobel at the end and a request for a photo.

All really enjoyed it. I did too. It wiped me out though and I am still recovering two days later. Not helped by insomnia—dreaming of floods and some unnamed, unspecified dread…

28th February 2020. Visit to Library: Up the tiny spiral staircase—glance to your left through a tiny cubbyhole to glimpse the Victorian raised roof. Then tour of all the treasures which include: musical legacy of earliest notation, to Elgar's baton for 1917 concert, Hooker's Ecclesia Polittie, Newton's works, Coronation of James II of 1685 (menus for which included Puffins, Pettitoes[1], Salamagundy[2]), Henry VIII's food requirements for visit to Worcester in 1510, illustrated vellum with doodles in the margins of two horses, tonsured knight, two griffins, an elephant like a giant pig with nose and hooves, 1450 English version of John Wycliffe's translation of the Bible, 13th century Vulgate Bible which is tiny made of gilt, gold leaf, lapis lazuli, Papal bulls, ms of St Isidore (8th century!), Greek papyri from 1st, 2nd and 3rd centuries, 14th century book of hours etc., etc., etc.

The room also contains lowered voices, warm atmosphere, old leather, gleaming tomes ceiling to floor, modern safety notices here and there. Six or seven volunteers working on delicate restoration—one translates medieval Flemish (on which Afrikaans is based). Large, thick cross beams mimic a Tudor aesthetic but are Victorian. Red covered tables with display units showing, almost casually, books of unrivalled uniqueness, importance, and beauty. England's

---

[1] *the feet of a pig used as food*
[2] *mixed greens with dressing*

(and others') history in one long, refectory-type room. Smells of leather, old paper, ancient ink. Modern desks with display drawers of untold treasures—Elizabeth I's, Mary I's, James and Charles I & II's signatures and seals. So close. One degree of separation from an iconic monarch.

Tea break, and we all get a cuppa and a biscuit, even me who has only expended energy in being curious and amazed. We have a long and interesting conversation about each volunteer's specialism. I am in awe at the wealth of talent and experience in that long room, all expending energy and time at conserving our joint heritage and culture.

Manuscript

His glad heart,
ten centuries old,
speaks to mine.

Tiny splashes reveal the shake,
the uncertainty of pen to parchment.
Then God's confidence takes over
and bold strokes seamlessly adorn the page.

Gold embraces turquoise.
It glitters on the giant letters
that curl hugely; painted,
important, kicking off
the serious square cut writing
that blackly fills the page.

We meet our man in the margins
where elephants with pig's trotters
and too thick, too short trunks, trundle.
Gryphons, dragons, birds and flowers
riot illicitly and here, a tiny lady,
hair coiled beneath a netted caul,
looks coyly over one pretty shoulder.

His touch was fresh then;
cold hands and frozen breath,
a sharp wind whistling,
crushed jewels glinting
and acrid ink, steaming from a brazen pot.

Across the dusty years
his act of grace still glows,
holds the light,

throws back his blessing.
And I, mute, am awestruck
at this holy inheritance,
this capture,
through the beauty of one man`s hand,
of infinite creativity.

Saturday 29th February 2020. Leap year! I am embedded in editing
the Song School poem and nothing is currently working. It's as if
every topic I try to cover is so rich that I do not know where to
start to get the metaphors rolling.

Thursday 12th March 2020. I am super excited and very gratified.
My Stations of the Cross poems will be printed, framed and
displayed around the Cathedral during Passion Week. Email from
Residentiary Canon, Stephen Edwards whom I have yet to meet, 'I
have now read all of the poems and they are really powerful,
beautifully crafted reflections which will be a blessing to many over
Holy Week. I am looking forward to seeing them framed and in
situ.' Ooooohhhhhh! This means so much to me.

I currently have lots of bits of paper with drafts of works in
progress and I am spending today ticking off jobs done and looking
forward to getting my head around work still to do. Onwards and
upwards!

Wednesday 18th March 2020. So far, I have not mentioned the
coronavirus. It has trundled along in the background, one issue
amongst many. But now it has escalated and become the matrix in
which we conduct ourselves, the stony fact around which we have
to calibrate our behaviour.

Amongst the fear and suffering that it brings is a tiny glint of
hope, the golden thread beneath the muddy path. It presents an
opportunity to change humanity's most damaging behaviours and
habits. We see, in Venice, fish and dolphins and swans already
returning to the waters due to lack of constant human pollution.

Nature doesn't hold grudges—given an opportunity, it will prosper. No flights equal no massive carbon emissions. We can eat local, we don't need all those trips, we can use our amazing connective technology to meet without all those environmentally damaging journeys. I know some journeys are necessary and that physical connection is important to all of us but there are some positives that can be gleaned from this. There's a chance of a bit of a reset, at least of priorities.

So, do I have a poetic response? Not yet. Things are changing daily and assumptions shift in line with that change. It's difficult to get a grasp of issues, challenges and responses and the life-implications thereof. Observations though:

The High street is emptier, people walk more mindfully and slowly, avoiding getting too close. This contributes to an atmosphere of awareness and feels like an improvement, as if we are all taking some kind of care of each other, with very little looking down at phones.

Another observation of a consequence of the pandemic is more local, social interaction—a WhatsApp group has been set up between residents on my street and it is providing a link of kindness and community.

Thursday 26ᵗʰ March 2020. We are currently on 'Lockdown' so apart from keyworkers, no one is allowed out apart from one hour for a daily walk/jog/cycle and vital supplies. Food shops are open but all others and pubs, cafes etc., are closed. I am currently pretending my kitchen is Boston Tea Party. I have made myself coffee and am now going to set to on the Song School poem. How glad am I that I have 'banked' all the Cathedral experiences: Library, Vergers, Undercroft, Song School, Poetry Workshop. The Stations of the Cross poems, although not going up around the nave, framed, will be shared widely on Facebook and Twitter posts from the Cathedral, day by day during Passiontide and may well reach a bigger audience that way.

I have sketched out a survival timetable to keep a grip (if only tenuous) on the slippery days—to include meditation, exercise, walk, contact and writing. Sounds like an Arvon retreat! There are pluses in this crisis—neighbours communicating with each other, the predominance of birdsong over traffic.

(Note from 2021—at this point the death toll had not started to rise in the UK and the NHS was not as under stress. I have to stress also, that I personally was not suffering as others did i.e., those who could not be with ill loved ones, those stuck in abusive relationships etc.)

We are learning how much we depend on each other, and especially depend on those who do not earn very much. We are learning that wealth doesn't really shield you, we are learning that there are resources to put social support in place and that the NHS, Social Care, police and transport should be priorities to fund, not opportunities to squeeze and scavenge. The white angels. I am getting solace from the FB Holy Communion from the Cathedral each day and the music ditto each evening.

Friday 27th March 2020. We are still in Lockdown. The weather continues amazing—the most brilliant and clear blue skies, warm sun and no clouds. Flowers are out and insects and birds are getting busy. Everywhere is so quiet, birdsong is easily heard and dominates every walk. Lovely. I took a long walk round the river and all I encountered respected the 2m rule. Many smiles of greeting too. Felt very mindful and caring. Let it continue once the virus goes.

Wednesday 1st April 2020. My Stations of the Cross have been posted—one a day—and have been received well, in the main. I am monitoring likes/loves and sad face emojis—keeping stats on the whole thing. That may be a bit obsessive, but I have never had the feeling so strongly for any piece of work of mine to be seen. I am proud of them.

The following is the intro I wrote that would have accompanied the framed poems that were to be mounted in the nave of the Cathedral. It still holds good:

Introduction to Stations of the Cross Poems

Movement is at the heart of the Stations of the Cross. We follow the footsteps one by one, we embody the journey and we empathise with the people in the story. We try to place ourselves in their shoes, feel their feelings as if for the first time, as they felt them.

It is a journey we ourselves replay—moments of temptation, moments of betrayal, moments of complete surrender and total loss, every day and over our whole lives. But this sequence shows we do not get stuck at any of the Stations. It is dynamic; we move on and keep moving, reaching the final Station, then moving beyond.

Stations of the Cross 1
Matthew 26 vs36-46 (Jesus in agony in the Garden of Gethsemane)

The Garden

Dusk, beneath the twisted trees,
thickens into night.
As the edges blur,
food and wine sit in the belly.
Eyes droop.

Heat still rises from the earth.
Insects chirrup.
Apart, he is motionless,
except sweat dripping under hair,
into eyes, joining tears.
He is a flood.

He knows how this must go.
It will roll out like a carpet onto the floor,
its story already woven.
But he needn't unfold it yet.
He could keep it under his arm
and steal away.

Doubt shakes him.
Doubt echoing from the beginning,
 when he sat empty, on a sun-sharp rock,
overlooking the world.
He was young and strong then.

While his friends sleep on, innocent,
prayer, deeper than fear
wrenches him from within.
A decision. A new birthing.

Stations of the Cross 2

Matthew 26 vs47-56 (Jesus betrayed by Judas and arrested)

Betrayal

In the end it was pure theatre.
Lights blazing through the thick dark,
glint of soldiers' metal and clink of swords.
A kiss of betrayal.

Jesus, almost weary,
almost humorous,
'Day after day I sat in the temple
teaching, and you did not seize me.'

Why then the kiss, Judas?
Everyone knows Jesus.
After all, he's the famous sensation,
followers throng, and crowds seethe.

I had to kiss him.
The Chief Priests insisted.
Not to identify him, you understand,
but to seal my own fate, brand me.
Easiest night's work, I thought.

So, we understand Judas.
Money is easy to understand, after all.
but it's the last line that's the killer:

'Then all the disciples forsook him and fled.'

That merry band travelling,
eating, drinking, healing,
catching fish and frying them,

feeding crowds,
forgiving, sharing, bonding.
Those guys. All of them.

Leaving Jesus,
surrounded by his enemies,
and the dark night.

Stations of the Cross 3
Matthew 26 vs59-66(Jesus condemned by the Sanhedrin)

Witness

The body writes the truth
every day, for all to see.
For those with eyes.

It cannot twist, edit,
translate, misinterpret,
be economical, decontextualise
or bear false witness.

It cannot lie.
An array of truths display
on our giveaway faces;
we tug an ear, look left,
pupils dilate, we squirm,
we blush, we grow pale.

It is witness.
It stands for something.
We lay it down, tie it up,
chain it to railings or trees,
glue it to pavements,
place it in front of tanks,
eyeball to eyeball.

More eloquent, then,
than men paid to garble and lie,
Jesus stands silent.

His body speaks,
unassailable, indivisible.
The Word.

Stations of the Cross 4

Mark 14 vs66-72 (Peter denies Jesus)

Peter

You don't run away completely.
You hang around, a sheep
searching for its shepherd.

But you can't hide your accent,
your hair, your clothes.
You stand out like a sore Galilean thumb.

You have been in a dream of your own grandeur,
your honour, your strength, reliability, toughness.
But the cock's crow in your ear
and your Lord's eyes upon you
show you your dreams are ash.

You were vainglorious, tempestuous, rash,
quick to follow, keen, big, rough,
a tough-looking fisherman, bearded.
Now, messy, hollow-cheeked, red-eyed
you break down and weep
when you hear his arithmetic come to pass:
three times a betrayal plus twice a cock crowing,
equals a man on his knees, in despair.

You aren't to know, then,
when you wake to that most wretched of days,
when food chokes you as much as your words do,
when all look askance at you,
when your fellow disciples, frightened too,
leave you to stew, you aren't to know
he will undo your three times table of betrayal
with such a sum of love, and more glory
than you could measure or deserve.

Stations of the Cross 5
Matthew 27 vs11-26, Mark 15 vs1-15, Luke 23 vs6-25, John 18
vs29-40 (Jesus judged by Pilate)

Crisis Management

You place me in an impossible position.
You do see that, don't you?
I am a representative of Rome,
upholder of its laws and might;
The Pax Romana.
I cannot allow you to disturb the peace.

I know, I know, my wife presses,
nay nags, me to release you;
a Righteous Man, she calls you.
And indeed, I see no crime in you.

What to do?
The crowd grows to a mob
and the mob has a voice:
Barabbas! it cries, Free Barabbas!
Now him, I do know,
nasty piece of work.
But you? You turn over a couple of tables
and speak of love.

I respect you.
Most men are on their bloodied knees
begging for mercy
but you are upright and calm.
You assume an equivalence.
Ha! I know, what a nerve!
But that takes courage
and I know that when I see it.
I need more time, do you see?

A couple of days, a week
to weigh the evidence, sift truth.
But the sun is high, tempers frayed
and Jerusalem is a-boiling.
Voices are baying from the dust,
whipping up fury,
so decisions have to be made.
You understand?
Looking into your eyes, I see you do.

What's that? Take down the sign?
No!
What I have written, I have written.
Leave him that.

Stations of the Cross 6
Mark 15 vs16-20, Matthew 27 vs27-31 (Jesus scourged and crowned with thorns)

Crown of Thorns

Ring a ring of roses
round and round we go.
Purple cloak, crown of thorns,
see the royal show!

Ring a ring a roses
mock what you don't know
spit and jeer and call him names
feel your hatred grow.

Ring a ring a roses
now we're in the flow
keep the rhythm going, lads,
blow on blow on blow.

Ring a ring a roses
one man on the ground
taking turns, one by one
round and round and round.

This is playground stuff, we know.
Bullies have their problems,
acting out fear through hate and cruelty.
How could they else given who they are,
how they are trained, how they are treated.
The bitten bites back.
The hated hates.

Except one man.
The one in the middle of the game.
Alone, deserted, derided,
clothed like a king, bleeding like a man,
he takes it all into his broken heart
and returns it with love.

Stations of the Cross 7
John 19 vs16-17 (Jesus takes up the cross)

A Quiet Day at Work

It's a quiet day for crucifying.
It's the festival, you see,
a bit of a holiday from death.
Normally.

We're good at this,
do it all the time.
Wood's prepared, ready,
possibly second hand
(we're thrifty too)
lined up in the yard round the back.

No splinters;
the grain rubbed,
stained with a stranger's blood,
whorls captured sweetly,
a proper carpenter's job.
Good strong, solid nails,
workmanship.

We have it down to a tee.
And if he can't carry it,
there's always onlookers,
grab a bystander,
make him carry it.
Always good for a laugh, that
the bloke's face!
when he thinks he'll be crucified instead.

That never happens, I might add.

We're efficient.
We have paperwork.
Three to do today,
a quiet day,
because of the festival.

Stations of the Cross 8
Luke 23 vs26-27 (Simon of Cyrene helps Jesus to carry the cross)

In from the Country

The noise. The crowds.
More people that I've ever seen.
Just in from the country,
excited to see Jerusalem.
My first time.

So I'm pulled along by the crowd,
through the food sellers, the kids,
the old men, the crying women.
Confused and, yes,
a bit curious.

Why pick on me?
Well, I know now.
I was the only young man around
and probably too slow and dazed
to get away.

Argue with the soldiers?
Are you mad?
I wouldn't argue with one Roman sword
never mind three.

But I could put it down, couldn't I?
Though I was worried for a bit
they'd get mixed up.
They laughed a lot at that,
those guards.

It was heavy, in that heat,
slick with blood.

Sweat in my eyes,
pain across my neck and shoulders;
it slipped from my grasp.

And he took it up again.

Stations of the Cross 9
Luke 23 vs27-32 (Jesus meets the women of Jerusalem)

The Green Wood

Now the streets burst.
It starts with one or two,
black robes billowing,
then five or six, until
a full murder of crows
gather to bewail the dead,
keening, howling.

But he is not dead yet
and still vocal.
First words since his trial
and he is implacably himself.

Women, cease your wailing!
Save your pity and your tears
for yourselves and Jerusalem.
It will not hold;
hate cannot last.
Mountains and hills
will cover its destruction.

See who I am?
I am your hope and future.
I am the green wood.

I am the green wood.

Stations of the Cross 10
Luke 23 vs33-38 (Jesus is crucified)

Perspective

Heat, dust and hungry birds circling;
cries of grief fade into the distance.
Just an occasional low sob
from my mother, my friends,
John.

Certainly a perspective from here.
All human woe and sin stretched out;
crying, gambling, mocking, spitting.
How can they know, blind as they are,
what they are doing?

Every muscle a torment, stretched and stressed,
every breath a heaving and gasping,
blood and sweat in my eyes,
lips and tongue cracked and splitting.
No way to move out of the pain.

The sky darkens and a wind picks up,
a tiny moment of balm.

A change.
Everything is change.
Give me strength for it.

Stations of the Cross 11
Luke 23 vs35-43 (Jesus promises the kingdom to the penitent thief)

He Sees the Men

The sun pounds down.
Birds wheel patiently
and flies gather to feast.
Dying,
his body twisted and broken,
he turns his head
one side, then the next.
He sees the men.

Right Side:
What's the fuss?
You're dying, like us,
like any thief, criminal, sinner.
If you were God, beloved,
you'd be out of this in a heartbeat
with your enemies dead in their armour
and we three on the open road
back to the cool North.
Go on! I dare you!
Free us all, O mighty one!
One last chance. Listen to me!
You have the power.
You choose not to use it.
FOOL.

Left Side:
I speak to you.
Life has dealt me a bad hand,
my father always said, a rotten apple...
but never mind, no excuses.

Here I am, a thief, a hard end,
deserving of it, sorry for it.
But you? What have you done?
I know of your deeds and they came from love.
I've heard your words and cannot find a bad one in them.
Show me, show me how to bear it.
I want to be like you, share your love,
find your peace.
Is it too late?

He turns his head one side, then the next.
He sees the men.
His heart breaks for them.
It breaks for us all.
Forgiveness rides his dying breath.

Stations of the Cross 12
John 19 vs25-27 (Jesus entrusts Mary and John to each other)

Of All Women

Of all women on the earth
she knows what is coming.
She knows the sword
will pierce her heart also.
She knows the price of love.
It was foretold. She was reminded often.
In her head, she knows all this.

But with her body, her animal body,
which bore this babe,
loved and fed and washed and held
this extraordinary child,
she does not know.

Bewilderment fogs her mind.
Not yet! Not now, not like this, not like this!
She turns to the others for answers.
There are no answers.

She needs a young man's arm
around her waist to hold her up,
so her grief does not fell her.
She needs a broad shoulder
to rest her burning forehead.
And he who always provided this
is ripped away,
killed in front of her.

The Jordan could not contain
all a mother's tears.

She could baptise the world with her sorrow.
She ages thirty years in one day.

His friend is there, next to her.
His arm holds her up,
his shoulder is damp from her weeping.
In the years ahead they would talk,
share, remember,
but for now
for now,
his mother clings to his beloved,
and they watch him die.

Stations of the Cross 13
Luke 23 vs44-46, John 19 vs28-30, Mark 15 vs33-39, Matthew 27 vs45-50 (Jesus dies on the cross)

Untitled

Three hours of darkness and we were glad of it.
All day we had watched, turned away, finally,
from the dying of the light in his eyes.

We did not see the earth quaking,
tombs opening, or the dead walking.
But we heard.
His cry, his drowning cry.

Another cry.
Finished. Done.

And a curtain is torn.
A chink, a crack, a rent,
crevice, window, door,
a rolled tombstone.

Thus his constant answer,
to the emptiness and the darkness,
is the YES of his body,
his love, his life.

Stations of the Cross 14
Matthew 27 vs57-61, Mark 15 vs44-47, Luke 23 vs50-56, John 19 vs38-42 (Jesus laid in the tomb)

Until

First chance we've had to think.
The day's heat slips away,
stars prick the sky
and deep shadows sharpen the boulder's edge.

You seem so near I could embrace you.
Then I see the sealed tomb
and you are immeasurably distant.

We thought all was lost before
but at least we had you in front of us;
could see, touch and hold your body.

Now we lock you away,
plant you in darkness,
and sit, watching.

Our faces are raw with tears.
Our fingers entwine.
We sit close, for warmth.
We sit here until.

Hope.
Despair.
Hope.

First Catch

(John 21 vs 9-14)

Beside the pale blue lake
I walk in dawn light
as I used to,
alone.

In the early hush
the long low flap of wings
breaks the calm of water
into glittering pieces.

As usual, the first catch
is kept aside for breakfast,
precious among busy men.

The chill stillness
disperses in the cooking smoke,
scatters at their chattering approach.
So far, the same.

'Who are you?
What are you doing?'
Fully frightened now,
clasping hands

'I am cooking for you,'
but there is no appetite
for today I am strange.

I smile and wait.
The fish is almost ready.

I am keeping up to date virtually with the Cathedral but it doesn't replace the real and transforming experience of sitting in that huge, hushed space. I walked past the south door yesterday and just listened. Behind the gate, the corridor and the thick door, I could hear the enormous, waiting silence. A giant, held, breath.

Now back to work: poem on Song School.

Wednesday 8th April 2020. Two weeks and a day of Lockdown. That manic upbeat energy that a crisis or emergency provokes in me has given way to a sort of slogging tiredness. I am waking up each night at about 3am then finding it hard to get to sleep again. I am trying to keep to a routine—one day a long two-hour walk, next day short walk and exercises. I don't want to forgo this structure because it feels like the only safe routine in my life. I am trying to fit writing around it, poems for Cathedral, Mercy (children's novel) and some Hive online work I've been asked to do. Add into this some long-deferred household tasks and you get quite a busy schedule. Perhaps I need some more chill time, during this anxiety. Though my long walks are very chilled during this time of anxiety. Birds seen—wrens, house martins, tits, seagulls, ducks, swans, a heron, moorhens and cormorants.

I listened again to the Cathedral. I didn't hear anything other than birdsong behind me on College Green and dry leaves whipped up by a tiny breeze. The sacred breath has contracted to a whisper of in and out in the crypt. It will revive like a bellows, don't worry. And bells will ring out splendidly and the choir will sing, Alleluia!

Tuesday 14th April 2020. I saw Easter in with online services from the Cathedral. Weather glorious. Also indulged in solo roast chicken and all trimmings on Easter Sunday cos it's special! Saturday was last day of Stations of the Cross series of poems and I have sent some other poems to Georgina for inclusion on Cathedral FB over the next few weeks—Song School, Ropesight and Verger poem.

Lockdown continues. The death tolls rises. I worry about my children.

21ˢᵗ April 2020. Fifth week of lockdown and self-motivation has become a real problem. I am managing physical exercise and tasks but creativity eludes me. Perhaps it's the oppressive sense of worry and the dominance of one appalling story day after day after day, with no relief. News bulletins and stories in between are completely overwhelming and I try only to listen to music. It feels like words chunk the world up inadequately and deceptively whereas the world, when encountered on walks, for example in the shape of a fishing heron, is more fluid and ungraspable.

And the Cathedral is closed and its FB page does not now feature a poem a day from me; that validated me to an extent. Now I have to write again. I'm not getting on with Mercy 3 (third in the trilogy of my children's novels) either—no café to sit in, to escape to, to give me a sense of purpose. I brood at the edges in my home and cannot concentrate.

But it is not all gloom. Mindfulness is the order of the day and it doesn't matter if a simple task takes forever. I have forever, at the moment. I can sit in a patch of sunlight in the front room carpet and stroke the cat and not worry. People are (mostly) careful of each other and there is less time on phones. People have to be careful not to bump into each other when out and about. I am in touch online with friends and family and that feels very precious. It is about now I would go and sit in the crypt and meditate. Too much TV at home and too little willpower to turn it off.

24ᵗʰ April 2020. Challenge accepted and completed i.e., get a Skype 'tea break' together for Hive colleagues. It is supposed to replicate the tea breaks at work, with chat and discussion but the main thread was 'can you see me?', 'I can't see anyone!', 'How do you turn the camera round?', 'You've all gone now,' etc., etc. Apparently Zoom is much better but I feel that's enough technology mastered for now.

I am still ending up at the Cathedral at the end of my walk—for a mixture of reasons—to touch the warm, ancient stone and check in with the building, to hear the comforting silence emanating, to reassure myself it's still there, to sit quietly in the beautiful College Green. I absorb the birdsong, warm breezes and play of light through the leaves of the trees. Normally I would be busily planning my poetic responses to something i.e., the effigies were going to receive the Amanda Bonnick treatment and I wanted to shadow and interview a member of the clergy here—Georgina or Stephen. But these plans are on hold, with no new input, and I am digging down into my own reserves of creativity. Feeling a bit fallow tbh, but that's OK, I think. There are momentous things happening in the world, and it feels too soon to have a creative response to them.

Friday 1ˢᵗ May 2020. The last week and a half since the previous entry has been quite up and down, mainly down. The sense of crisis, that occasioned a great deal of energy and positive action, has dissipated into an ongoing long doom and gloom of worry (especially re my children and how they are coping. They are such impressive young adults, but I can't help but worry). My creative cup is empty. I try to sit to write a new poem and it won't happen. I need input. I don't want to write about the virus. It's too close. I have no perspective on it. I have no metaphor for it because I'm living it and it is enough in itself to deal with. I have no lessons to draw from it. I am sure the above will come. Good work will emerge and some kind of reckoning and assessment will take place. But for now I turn the dial to R3 or R6 to avoid constant news. I read, watch TV and keep active. I miss the Cathedral and visit its outside every day and hear it chiming the hour. Can't wait to hear its peals again.

6ᵗʰ May 2020.

15ᵗʰ May 2020. Apparently nothing happened on 6ᵗʰ May!
    Bit of a change—Cathedral is starting to open up slowly (unfurling like a flower, outside petals first, until the inner leaves unfold); the undercroft work is underway again, the Dean et al are allowed to film communion from inside the Cathedral. I will be

having some more poems up on FB.

So how am I? The last week has felt a bit like it has unravelled. Not doing my resolutions, going to bed late, too much TV, sleeping in til 9am. I'M TURNING INTO A TEENAGER!

Any creativity has taken a dive. No input equals no output. I am trying to push on Mercy 3 but only squeezing out 300-500 words every other day. No poetry is emerging.

Why? Combination of factors, some of which you'd think would be conducive to writing i.e., lots of time, solitariness, no need to be available to anyone, BUT lots of time just bleeds into everything. Productive work results best from clear parameters and deadlines. Too much solitariness can become loneliness, isolation and depression. On the plus side (there's got to be one somewhere!) I am re-grouping mentally, getting to know myself and my particular priorities. I am in my body—walking, observing and enjoying nature which is lush and lovely at this time of year. What if this continues? I think I'll need to get a little stricter with self and think of some strategies to trick myself into writing.

I miss the Cathedral. Its tall ceiling, its soaring vaults, its jewel-like windows, its gold and white crypt where all mysteries are kept.

I miss the Hive and colleagues there and the banter, and the regular customers (good and bad!), the work, the books, the silences, the noisy children—all of it!

I have, in my work at the Cathedral, attested to the links to history contained in the building itself, the ancient ceremonies, and the various activities of stonemasons, bellringers, musicians, each one echoes from down the years. During lockdown I pass the Cathedral every day. It is quiet, silent, unmoving, no rustling, clanking, voices, heaters humming. And I have come to realise that what makes it living, important, is not only its wonderful links to and foundation in its past and history, but also its living breathing community who love it and the church and who gather and go, come together and leave, visit, stay, visit, like shining beads of mercury on a tray, coming together, splitting apart, coming together again.

2nd June 2020. So, a couple of weeks have passed since the last entry. Days are not divided up into 'work' days and 'rest' days, so they tend to merge. What also happens is that within one day, tasks are done at different times than usual; meal times are fluid, exercise can be taken in the morning, writing (normally an afternoon activity for me) can pop up anytime. A thread of the connective tissue of social media winds through the day, apart from those moments when I cannot bear to hear any more news and commentary about news. It is death, illness, government corruption, lies and deceit, and now hideous racial violence and terrible crackdowns on peaceful protests in America. I have to put on the music and dance, cry or just listen. Faves include: Paul Simon, Kate Bush, Fleetwood Mac, George Michael, Andrea Bocelli. All keeping me going.

And now my daughter is here, back from Uni, from her corona-free bubble in London, to my corona-free bubble in Worcester. Sooo good to have a hug! So lovely to talk at length with another human being, especially such a perceptive, wise and interesting one as she is. So great to go for a walk and then sit in the shade under a tree by the river. We also rescued a baby seagull which had fallen two storeys from its nest in College Green. She'll be here for a week at least, maybe two, so I'll have to make the most of her.

I haven't written a poem for over four weeks. It's just not happening. The oracular flow has ceased to pour. On the plus side my poems for the Cathedral FB page have been up and garnered a few likes and comment. The Ropesight poem struck a chord (sorry!) with the bellringers and the Bellringer in Chief, Mark Regan, wants to submit it to Ringing Times, the bellringing magazine, which is very gratifying. It is also published in the Cathedral newsletter, so more coverage!

Monday 22nd June 2020. Today the Cathedral opened for private prayer (nave only), 1pm-3pm daily. I was among the first and when I got to the North door, the Bishop, the Dean and Chaplains were outside, the bishop talking to reporters and camera crew. Georgina was there and she greeted me at a safe distance and it was wonderful to chat and connect after all this time.

I went into the cool, airy space of the nave; no pews, only chairs spaced two metres apart and signs on the rows indicating where to sit. I sat. A gentle breeze from behind me, through the wide-open West door, with its snapshot view of the Cathedral garden, steps and ultimately the river, wafted over my skin, made me feel welcome.

Looking ahead of me, the altar was simple, with an unadorned large golden cross on top. It glowed in the beam of sun from above and lit up the space around. It was a good focal point on which to rest my eyes, while my mind unpacked its burdens, one by one, and laid them in a hot, angry, sad, messy, woebegone heap in front of the cross. The enormous sense of a worry shared, a weight lifted and borne, a wider view than that of my ego being offered me, a truly kaleidoscopic panoramic view of time forward, time backward and time present, spreading like a golden meadow of wildflowers around me.

I stood, bowed, and went to the altar, where I lit a candle for all of us; those hardly touched by any sorrow, those whose lives have been shattered and near destroyed, those who are exhausted and near collapse, those who have died. All of us. Those angry with the government, those scared of the future, those excited by new challenges, those who see us standing at some half-open door of possibility and change.

11th August 2020. A bit of a gap between the last entry and this— filled with going back to work in real life, trying to adapt to the new strictures at the Hive, the constant hand-washing, the distancing, the mask-wearing for an eight hour shift, and the quarantining of all returned books, the reminding customers of the new rules, the track and tracing of everyone coming in through the big glass doors. I feel like a shepherd with her sheep and I am constantly reminding and gently chiding customers etc.

Also, I have been busy devising and presenting Poetry on Form for the Hive, a ten-week series explaining and exemplifying different poetic forms. It has been fun, though! As well as getting other poets together to do Poetry in Motion for the Hive online offer too.

So, now I am in the Cathedral, having a cuppa and a cheese sandwich. Almost feels like back to normal. I am currently post-zoom launch of *Call and Response* which is a pamphlet of poems by local poets who were asked by me to contribute their poetic responses to Worcester Cathedral. This was originally planned as a live event with members of the public invited but ended up on Zoom cos of You Know What. It went well though and the pamphlet looks grand. I look forward to it being sold in the Cathedral bookshop when that is possible. Most of the poets attended plus Polly, Tony, and Rod of Black Pear Press. Georgina said some lovely words about the project and, very pleasingly, about the Stations of the Cross poems. At the end of the evening Polly, Nina and Ruth stayed on screen and we all had quite a long chat. Felt like old times.

Now I have to solidify my plans for the remainder of the residency; poems about Women in the Gospels, interviews with Georgina and other canons, the writing up of this journal. Question to self: am I going to be brave enough to include my own religious/spiritual journey in the narrative? next question: What can I call the book, now the title *Call and Response* has been taken?

Faces and pictures emerge from the stone walls of the Chapter House (where I am drinking this cuppa)

- a man with 3D glasses on or alternatively the muscled six pack torso of Zeus
- a skull-like spectral profile of a hag, with a small black bear cub, rubbing noses.
- a sorrowful early black and white photo of Jesus
- Dominic Cummings' bald head, to the eyes, spookiest of all.
(actually, these are remnants of painted walls)

28th August 2020. I've just been reading though the Gospels to find traces of women (research preparatory to poems about them) and have certainly got a very different perspective and reaction to all the crowd scenes. 5000! How are they all distancing? And if properly spread out, how can they possibly hear Jesus' words? Chinese whispers to the guy at the back.

Thinking about the final part of my residency and the WiG poems (Women in Gospels), I really want them to be a counterbalance to the dark, intense Stations of the Cross poems. I want to explain the written stories, mentions, asides, assumptions but also explore the invisible and inaudible lives of the women: who are there but how, when? I appreciate the dangers of exercising imagination and poetic licence in this way, so I intend to ground any poems on the text itself and on believable historical probability. I'm no Gospel scholar but I do read widely around this: Richard Bauckham's *Gospel Women*, Carla Ricci's *Mary Magdalene*, Geza Vermes's *Jesus the Jew* and others) I also credit my own heart response.

9th September 2020. There's an autumn nip in the air and a new term feel to everything. Time to buy new stationery, methinks. I am deep in the research for the women and with each one, each strong, very individual woman, I fall in love with them and want to honour them. What exceptionality must have existed for them to have stood out against the silent and invisible women who were not written about, not given their own voice. Scholars acknowledge that for a woman to be named in Gospel discourse she had to be important in the early, establishing church. The Gospel writers were writing within living memory of Jesus (at least the documents we have are between 70 and 100 years from Jesus' life but that's not to say that oral tradition and earlier documents weren't circulating much closer to his lifetime) so any women who had become important in church, whose names were known and probably famous, could not have been omitted. So, if any women are name-checked in the Gospels, you can be sure they are important and well-known. My journal may be a little neglected as I immerse myself in first-century Palestine, all the noises, smells and colours and voices.

17th October 2020. A beautiful, crisp, sunny, definitely autumn day. Leaves of unbelievable colours; bright gold lighting up pavements, deep rich reds of blood and royalty, browns of such a depth they could be flower beds, and those still green, hopeful and in denial. A glorious mediaeval tapestry of Englishness. I could almost glimpse a white hart, standing stock still, ears pricked, velvet nostrils quivering, between the slender trunks of the beeches.

All feels as if it is slowly coming to an end. Two more series of poems (ministry poems, Women in Gospels poems). I have meetings with Georgina, Michael and Stephen next week to discuss their experience of ministry and vocation. Also, to talk to Georgina about the 'winding down' of the residency. Sad.

28th October 2020. Wednesday. In Boston Tea Party (hurray!) So, some domestic good news (I have been without a boiler for three weeks, having to shower etc., every other day at my bubble's house at great inconvenience to them)—my new boiler is to be installed tomorrow. The chimneys (which have been covered and repointed, to achieve which the house has been covered in scaffolding for over a month) have been finished so I feel a bit better. These issues have been worrying but now I can at least be warm and clean.

The above is personal stuff but has been a bit of a gloomy backdrop to my life lately. Thank heavens there's a bit of sun on the horizon. Also, I was really buoyed up after last week's meeting with Georgina. She was positive about the residency so far (even with all the event planning that had to go south due to the pandemic) and was really appreciative of the poetic contribution to the Cathedral's online offer throughout lockdown. She feels it should be prolonged until next April, after Easter, so that Stations of the Cross can be displayed Easter 2021, framed and in the nave, as was originally intended. Also, so that we can have a final, celebratory live event in real-time in a physical location. This is also prolonged so that there is a certain degree of compensation for time lost during lockdown, and as a thank you. I was very moved by this and felt appreciated. Time to get on with the tasks ahead.

12th November 2020. Time has moved on and I am feeling blocked re the Mary Magdalene poems. I need to loosen up about it, approach them from a different angle. Or perhaps flex my muscles on the other women. This time last year I was cooking with gas in the face of what seemed a greater challenge i.e., writing a series of poems about the Stations of the Cross. I was also rather daunted by the task, but I had my seat in the café where I could imaginatively enter into 1st Century Palestine and go wherever my mind wanted to, listen attentively to the voices that emerged. Now I am stuck in my house, with only myself and the ongoing stress of being in the middle of the biggest pandemic since the 14th Century. I am also stalled because I love these women and want to do them justice. I need to find the freedom from the need to be the 'definitive' portrait.

Btw, we are in a 2nd less restrictive lockdown and the Cathedral has closed except for prayer. It is still online though. There are still cars about, people in town, Hive open, so it doesn't feel like the first lockdown. Lockdown Lite, if you will.

17th November 2020. Am I blocked?! I feel blocked!! ARgggh! I made a massive mistake of joining a poetry FB page that has the aim of writing one poem a day for a month, with a prompt each day. Now I feel more blocked than ever, plus distracted, plus a failure. I need to mentally clear the decks, focus down microscopically and with love on the great joy of trying to uncover a little of the faces of these women. Let myself be a channel.

Also, btw, happy birthday to my mum who died three years ago and would have been 85 today. We used to have a family tradition that if it snowed on her birthday (I guess it did back in the 60s and 70s) it would be a white Christmas. I can report it has not snowed.

7th January 2021. The pandemic is too huge a remit for this particular book to cover but it is also something impossible to ignore. It affects every aspect of life and feels like a constant sense of emergency, triggering adrenalin which has nowhere to go. We are mainly powerless at this time, so our adrenalin isn't used in action or to control events. We remain stressed and on alert. This leads to constant tiredness and an almost debilitating depression. Many people are also dealing with loss, bereavement, illness, unexpected childcare, loneliness, lockdown with disability, lockdown with abusers etc. There are as many examples of suffering as there are people.

I am, for the main, not too badly affected. True, I did not see friends at Christmas, and I couldn't see my son or his wife, but I am healthy and still in work. The library remains open and feels a safe place to work so I benefit from the team spirit, presence and cheer of all of my great colleagues.

Where I am not doing well (and you, dear reader, may have guessed this already) is creativity. I am finding writing very difficult. What is so very frustrating about that is that I have time and opportunity aplenty to sit down and write but I feel the need, constantly, to be doing something practical. So, I am having to be very disciplined, to sit down at home, and write amid all distractions. This feels almost impossible. Perhaps because the flip side of the outpourings of creativity is the need for it to be fed, for the spring to be replenished by external stimuli. And those are thin on the ground at the mo.

12th January 2021. I am finally getting some drafts of the Women in the Gospels poems together (known, in my shorthand as WiG). Thank God, I hear you all cry, perhaps now she can stop moaning on about being blocked. I have realised that one of the blocking factors not previously recognised is that the language of the Bible is heartbreakingly beautiful and iconic in its own right. I do feel a little like, 'who am I to try to add to this glory?' but hey ho, that's what every generation of writers does and if it is rubbish, it will fall down behind the sofa of obscurity and be forgotten for ever. So that's a blessing.

Introduction to the Women in the Gospels Poems

If you have read so far you will know the difficulties I have faced (or made for myself) in writing the following series of poems. I hope you enjoy them. The research I did was based on *The Common Bible* (The Revised Standard Version 1973), *Gospel Women* by Richard Bauckham (Eerdmans, 2002) and *Mary Magdalene and Many Others* by Carla Ricci (Augsburg Fortress, 1994), plus my own reading of authors such as Richard Rohr, Geza Vermes and others, plus the inevitable Google Search. I conducted a very small and totally non-representative survey on FB amongst my friends with the question, 'What does Mary Magdalene mean to you?' and some very interesting and varied answers popped up, some of which informed my poems about her. I have included the bible reference where appropriate in case you want to go back to the story to see how I got to where I did.

Oil and Tears

Luke 7 vs36-50

I

I reach the middle of the room, reds and blues hanging on the walls, oil lamps lighting every staring eye, rich food spreading like an invitation on a vast table, aromas of meats and sauces wrapping themselves around me. I see clothes of unimaginable colour and cleanliness, starched and elegant, grand enough to be worn by angels. But I cannot see my own faded robe, my market stall bangles and shabby ribbons. My eyes are drawn to you, where all the paths of light lead.

And the tears are starting, rising up from the deepest well of love and gratitude, through the earth, through my dusty naked feet and up, up into my centre. I am filled again and again; where else can the living flood emerge but from my eyes? You tell me I am forgiven, that I am changed now and all my hurts are healed, so I want to heal you, from the shadow of the hurt to come, with this great healing spring of life. I kneel and tributaries swell to rivers as I weep at your feet.

I can't stop and my hair blots away what it can. I reach for my jar and break open the lid. In that close room it exudes a cloud of the sweetest, lightest fragrance. It spills amidst my tears and onto your feet. My long dark hair tangles about my face and I use it to soak it all up, as tenderly as a mother wipes her child's face. But I am a waterfall. In that thunderous roar I cannot hear the excited start of gossip; and between the curtains of my hair, I cannot see the lascivious fascination pick up and spread like a tiny chain of wicked flames.

II
Side-eye from Simon,
the Pharisee.

Everything in place; food, drink,
guest list, discreet lighting,
beautifully laden table, polished silver,
rich smell of the cooked meats rising.

All arranged;
introductions, light chat,
a few stories, gentle questions,
then a little tougher, put him on the spot,
sound him out.

But this.

How did she get in?
I'll have to have words with the staff.
How dare she approach my guest,
in my house, at my dinner. Ruined.

That woman, weeping and weeping,
touching him with her dirty hands,
her hair, her lips.
Who knows where she's been.
I could guess. I know her type.

III
Simon, I hear you. You, who give me no embrace, who keep stiffly
from me, nervous of my touch and of your own. I arrive and you
give me nothing. While you count your spoons, Simon, she has not
ceased to kiss me. While you check your wine, she breaks her fine
flask and anoints me. You do not anoint my head with any welcome
but she has anointed me with precious oil. You give me no water to

85

wash the street off my feet, but she has soaked my feet with her
tears. You give me no linen, but she dries my feet with her hair.
Hush, Simon. Who, between you, loves me best? I know her. She is
oil and tears, hair and kisses, gratitude and courage. She is all love.
And I am all forgiveness.

Woman Healed of a Haemorrhage

Matt 9 vs18-22
Mark 5 vs22

Never clean.
Worse, always unclean.
Twelve dragging years
of constant pain, constant blood,
washing, washing, washing.

No burden to wait, therefore,
wait outside his house.
I've waited so long.
Despite the huge crowd,
no one waits near me.

I won't beg or plead
or embarrass him.
Just a touch of his clothes
will be enough, I know.
He won't even know I'm here.
So I catch the fringe of his gown,
time it as he passes,
when the crowds thin away from me
and surge in front of him.

But he turns.
He calls me daughter.
Tells me to take heart.

In that throng, that press,
he feels my thin fingers
briefly touch his hem.
And then my body is warm for the first time

and that stale smell has gone
and my womb no longer weeps.
Now flesh clothes my bones,
I am no longer shunned,
and every now and then,
I even dance in the sun.

Feeding of the Five Thousand

John 6 vs1-14

Well, we lost all the baskets.
Twelve good woven baskets,
tough, they were, useful,
wood, skins, washing.
Not all mine, of course,
quite a few lent.

I told them: People will just take them,
you've given them free stuff already,
they'll just assume.
And they did.

Can't afford new ones.
Can't ask! How can I?
Leave the food to me, I'd said, women's work.
Never imagined the numbers. Who would?
I ran around that day, I can tell you,
but no go. No food anywhere at such short notice.
Mortified to ask him.
But he turned it around, as he always did.
And we were all fed.

No, it was not thousands!
Enough though.
Enough to be a miracle.

Joanna

Luke 8 vs3

Welcome, welcome!
My home is not as grand as it used to be,
but never mind!
My welcome is warm, just for you.
You are here now and we can talk.
I can finally tell you what my life was like.

My first life was of golden cups, plentiful high-sauced food,
of slaves attending, of soft linen, pungent perfume,
oils and butter, expensive wine.
And the people I moved among;
Royalty and high-born Romans,
high priests and rich merchants;
power, influence and persuasive charm.

But beneath the luxury was a charnel house,
our old town of Rakkath,
a city of bones, of defilement, and decay.
We negotiated with death every day,
desperate to fulfil the whims of a childish despot
thousands of miles away.
None of us could lift up our heads,
and under the weight of those daily bargains with power,
my spirits began to sink.

Chuza, my high-flying husband,
turned his blind eye to these accommodations.
A hard worker, though, top of his tree,
and Herod called on him at every turn.
But this tree was dead at the roots and I could smell it,
above the receipts, the affidavits, invoices,
a slow smell of rot.

So I sank
all my joy, song, waywardness, happiness, optimism,
slowly dripped down those fine Roman drains
into the defiled Jewish earth beneath
and I became an empty ghost.
I did not eat—why would I?
I could not sing—where was joy?
With every lowered look, every concession,
every shibboleth shrugged off; my life ebbed.
My tide was full out,
leaving stinking corpses on the shoreline.

A grim picture, ne?
Chuza's despair took me through the market,
with a whiff of the grave, no light in my eyes,
hopeless, loveless and godless.
He had heard of Jesus, his healing,
 and on that brisk, salt-laden Galilean day,
I was pushed forward.
'Joanna, he might help' he pleaded.
And now I am thinking,
'Oh, Chuza, be careful what you wish for!'

Then though I felt no whirlwind, saw no dove,
heard no roaring fire.
His eyes met mine and he smiled.
His hand rested on my head.
'I see you, sister,' he said, 'I hear you.'

And all the bolted doors in my heart
clanged open and love rushed through me;
my soul danced for joy
in the dusty sand of the marketplace.
I don't know how I ended up on my knees—
Chuza was embarrassed—

'Think of your dress! Don't make a scene!'
but I did.
'Lord,' I said, 'I have need of your healing.'
'You are healed,' he said, 'by your knowing.'

That was it.
What turned in my heart that day?
A Scythian's arrow, swift and inevitable,
reaching the tock of its target,
could not have been more precise,
more instant.

I smiled in return.
The words came before any thought.
'How can I serve you?'
'Follow me,' he said, 'I have use of you.'

Use of me.
So that was what I needed all along.
To be of use.

Jairus's Daughter

Luke 8 vs49-56

In and out of fever,
no sense anywhere,
walls moving
as I breathed.
Fire scorched me.

Voices around me
crying and wailing.
From the other room
laughter somewhere
mocking.

In the dark, alone,
wanting my mother,
waiting for her touch,
her voice.

Whose voice pulled me back
as I drifted away?
I don't know
but he called me 'little girl'.
And called for food.

I was no baby, I told him,
later,
I was fully twelve,
nearly a woman.

But I was glad of the meal.

Pilate's Wife

Matthew 27 vs19

I know that dreams matter.

Most dreams are fragments,
tatters that drift
like wisps of ash
in the waking day.

But this was sharp, clear,
and told itself over and over
however much I woke then slept,
then woke again.

This man, this Jew,
whom I saw for an instant,
shuffling between the pillars,
between his beating and his gaol,
one glimpse up through blood-dripping hair,
I aghast at the mess of him,
he steadily gazing.

Printed on my mind and replayed
through my hot and disturbed nights.
It must mean something,
that look, that look,
that look of forgiveness.

Peter's Mother in Law

Mark 1 vs24-31

Knock, knock!
Who's there?

Peter and a few friends,
and we need food
and wine and possibly
somewhere to crash tonight…

Yes, that's me, first mother-in-law joke
as well as first healing.
By that man,
the one who stole Peter from me,
stole Peter from my daughter.
Mixed feelings don't begin to describe.

Two verses I get:
'Lying sick with a fever then
the fever left her and she rose and served them.'

Couldn't wait, those boys.
Busy, organising, planning, excited.
No time—or skill!—to cook or serve.
So that's where I came in.
Not that I'm ungrateful.
He did heal me, after all.
Just would have liked a bit of a rest first, that's all.

Woman Taken in Adultery

John 8 vs3-11

The Set Up
Someone was watching, someone snitched, someone close to her, someone consumed with envy, someone with a grudge, someone betrayed her. Nasty.

The Scene
A crowd, listening to the teaching. Then she's pulled to the centre of the crowd, who recognise her, sense a different turn of events, start taking sides. The elders want him to condemn her. Really, really want him to. Tension rises.

The Trap
First, he ignores them. Leans down to write on the ground with his finger, concentrates on this, focuses. The crowd wonders: is he indifferent to the rising voices, is he playing for time, is he composing his answer, is he managing the growing violence by slowing it all down?

The Trap Reversed
He stands suddenly, low to high in a moment. And says it: He who is without sin, let him throw the first stone. The reflecting mirror of true compassion shines back on the crowd and they see their own greedy faces, see their hearts as stained with wrongdoing as any they accuse. They trickle off, one by one, grumbling, like children denied a game.

Jesus resumes his writing on the ground.
He is making a point.
Making them wait.
Slowing it down,
calming the breath,
clearing the mind,
shifting the focus,
letting them wander off,

no more to see.

The men leave.

The woman remains.
He looks up:
'Where are they?
Does no one condemn you?'

Her only uttered words:
'No one, Lord.'
He too does not condemn
but goes further. He forgives.
And further. He instructs.
'Do not sin again.'

She does not die that day.
She is given back to life,
to make her choices
perhaps to sin again
for life is long and memory short.
But forgiveness and love are infinite,
and the fingers make the words in the sand
and the sun reaches the height of the sky
and the circling vultures flap away, disappointed.

Mary Magdalene

The Healing

'Happy the man whose children are male
and woe to the man whose children are female.'
Ecclesiastes

My gifts had turned to demons.
How else, with this?

I was a sufferer not a sinner.
Demons.
Not sins.

I had the full complement.
A compliment really
Seven needed to subdue me.

One day this voice, next day that,
noisy, powerful, challenging.
Seven different maps,
with seven different destinations.
No one in charge
and no room for me.

Some days my family's love soothed me,
silenced the fractious navigators.
Other days their surveillance angered me
and all seven shouted wicked words,
mouthpieces of mischief, hurting those I loved.
I was shunned
and my life mapped out in misery.

He saw through all that.

Saw them, named them,
dismissed them.
Flipped their energy
and gave me back my power.

All that was left was a charred place,
a whiff of smoke and ash.
Healing rained down
and I became garden
of spring flowers.

And I grew and grew
beyond my family
beyond my birthplace
beyond the angry faces
beyond all the fences and walls.
I grew out into the world,
out into time.

Mary Magdalene

Who do you say that I am?
Some say I met the Emperor of Rome
on my travels, who egged me on,
caught me red-handed,
guilty of being right.[3]

Some call me a whore
in words and paint and film;
Mel Gibson's take is Monica Belluci,
smudged mascara and sexy hair.
Caravaggio, Piero di Cosima, Holbein,
all chip in, lubricious voyeurs,
me, exotic, hair flowing, dangerous.

I am not your convenient opposite,
your history's harlot,
soft repository of sinful fantasy,
male sins atoned by my tears,
my hairshirt, my ashes,
my naughty glint in the eye.

Don't set me up against the other Mary,
whiter than white Mother.

I know, a dichotomy always holds
the circling devils outside the homestead,

---

[3] *Mythical tale: "According to tradition, Saint Mary Magdalene gained an audience in Rome with the emperor after the Crucifixion and Resurrection of Christ. She denounced Pilate for his handling of Jesus' trial and then began to talk with Caesar about Jesus' resurrection. She picked up a hen's egg from the dinner table to illustrate her point about resurrection. Caesar was unmoved and replied that there was as much chance of a human being returning to life as there was for the egg to turn red. Immediately, the egg miraculously turned red in her hand."
(Monastery Icons: https://rb.gy/uamzjd retrieved 2021)*

but it paints us false and limits us both.

In truth, I am what all people are.
I hold within me the sum of my choices.
Don't simplify, don't patronise,
don't explain away.
We are all paradox,
all travelling,
changing,
growing.

Shedding old skins.

Mary Magdalene

Who am I?

I am the healed woman
who was turned around,
who followed, who supported,
who worked, who stayed,
who travelled, who stayed,
who stayed, who stayed,

who stayed outside Sanhedrin,
outside Pilate's palace, following
through roiling streets,
collapsing at the cross,
negotiating with guards,
finding Joseph of *Arimathea,*
cleaning and wrapping his body.

Tomb then tombstone.
Then dark.
Two long nights of dark.

Never leaving.
Earthquake, stone rolling,
guards wailing.

And him. And his voice.
Mary.
Rabboni.

And then all the bells of heaven
ringing in my ears, and then running,
running, skirts flapping,
veil streaming, tears drying.
Good news! Good news! Best news!

And telling it ever since.

Mary Clopas

John 19 vs25

Take shape, Mary Three.
Step forward from the shadows
and unwind your veil.
Break from the dark
into the sunlit garden
and let us see your smiling face.

Tell us if we're right,
on our detective trail.
First Clue: Clopas.
You are the mother of Simon,
Simon who is the son of Clopas
which is backwardspeak for:
you are the wife of Clopas.

Second Clue: Clopas is the brother of Joseph.
The Joseph, husband of Mary,
father of Jesus.
By my reckoning, which I admit may be a little crooked,
this makes you Jesus' aunt.

This theory I like; I am an aunt.
You get to be cool,
a grown up and a friend,
a refuge from parents,
a confessional,
a sounding board,
an ally and an alternative.

I so want this to be true.
Even if it isn't
we do know you were there, Mary Three,

until the end.
True, brave and loyal,
best qualities of an aunt.

Mary Mother of Jesus I

"We are all meant to be mothers of God, for God is always needing to be born."
Meister Eckhart

Epitome of obedience,
head bowed, accepting,
you empty yourself
to be filled by God.

But what if…

What if you are the spirited girl
who scrapes her knees,
on the hard rocks in the mountains,
who chases the goats
to hear their bells clang,
who twiddles her long, untidy hair
into scrappy ringlets as she watches
stars wheel in the sky and cluster thickly
over the milk warm waters of Galilee?

What if you are the girl who argues every toss?
Who exasperates her parents
with her quick backchat,
then makes them laugh
with her funny faces and wild dancing.
What if you are the girl who can swim a mile
further than your brothers,
can persuade the stubborn donkey to move
with whispered love words in its velvet ears,
who can spin a plate longer than a song,
who can knit and sew badly
yet still surprise a sister with a robe
made secretly and with love.

Who escapes the town whenever she can
to visit the herdsmen and animals
to watch the fish gleaming, leaping,
in the drop-shaking nets hauled from the lake.

This girl who cannot sit still enough
to write her own name:
Miriam, Miriam, Miria, Miri, Mir,
then she's off and out to follow the ring
of winter riming across the folds of the land,
to watch the hawk stone dropping onto the mouse.

This girl. This.
This spirit.
This energy.

Who recognises her purpose,
who gathers her courage—
salty, peppery, spiced by wit—
and bows her head
to what feels like her life story,
what feels like our life story,
to open her heart
to what she knows all along
exists beneath, behind,
within, every single living being.

Mary Mother of Jesus II

The Dangers of Art
Madonna:
Seated, blue-robed,
head-covered, baby-cradling,
face tilted down, filled with love,
a warm cocoon,
safe, secure.
That perfect triangle loved by artists;
Roman reliefs, Book of Kells,
Botticelli, Fra Filippo Lippi.
How lovely each Madonna is,
a dot to dot of each century's female character and beauty:
sinless, pure, serene,
angelic, detached remote.

Pieta:
The German word is 'vesperbild',
that moment of sunset
when the sun slips away.
And Mary, seated,
blue-robed, head-covered,
blood-spattered, hair-tattered,
cradles the dead body of her son.
Her gown billows around them both,
no protection.
Her face is lifted in grief,
eyes brimming,
her whole body a cry,
a stretch towards heaven
and a tender covering.

'O, Woman.'

Syro-Phoenician Woman—Matthew 15 vs21-25

Ask anyone, it's what I do.
I answer back.
I don't take 'no'.
And that day I was desperate.

My daughter, light of my eyes,
was sick and suffering.
She's such a sweet one:
'the teaching of kindness is on her tongue.'
I couldn't lose her.

So, I approached him,
begged him, implored him.
I could see he was tired,
could see his disciples' concern,
but when would I get this chance again?

Then he said he was not sent for me,
only for the House of Israel.
So that was that.
Only it wasn't.
I persisted.

I may be simple but that didn't make sense.
I knew his love was for everyone,
how could it not be?
I told him I'd take even the crumbs
from under the table

Brought him up short, that did.

He turned and looked at me properly.
'O, woman,' he said,
my heart sank, for my husband
often said that to me,
'Be it done for you as you desire.'
and then my heart took flight.

We both learned something:
I that faith has restored my daughter
(and that persistence pays off),
he that his ministry is for everyone
and for all the world.

Quite a day.

Salome I

Based on the extra-canonical text, Psalm of Thomas 16

I am a tower
on the doubled rock
of Truth and Mercy.

Angels hew my stones.
Charity carves my roofbeams.
Faith instates its door,
whose unlocked key
is my single Mind.

Who enters here, rejoice.
Who leaves, have hearts full
of gladness unto the top.

My undivided tower is built anew
for thee; anesh of storax,
incense in the palm,
smokes forth, a clouded jewel.

Mayest thou answer, Jesus.
Mayest thou hear, Jesus.
Garland me with brightness
and wonder at my single,
diamond-pure nature.

For I am not double-minded.
One is my heart, one my intent.
Take me up unto the House of Peace.
For there is no thought in me, but for thee,
no thought that is split or twain.
All of me in one, and that is thine.

Salome II

Every story needs a teller,
every teller a witness
and I am both.

Known for knuckling down
getting on with it
helping where I can.

Midwife to The Word,
aunt to the Saviour,
sister to a holy cuckold.

The family forgave him
in the end. Families do.
And she was pretty, nice
and in trouble.

So much fuss
but he was born easy
and all were gladdened.

Bonny he was,
good as gold,
his mother's heart

and his aunt's.

He grew and knew himself
his strength, his source.
Outgrew his little family.

We knew, didn't we?
The ending?
So much love,
it never ends well.

Woman of Samaria at the Well

John 4 vs1-30

Drawing Water from a Well
He shocks with his sharp shadow
across her dusty feet.
She is leaning over the top of the well
reaching for the wooden bucket.

Tiny stones drop into the blackness,
echoing into the deep.
He sits at the side of the road,
weary, tired and alone.

He shocks her again when he speaks.
She looks around. What should she do?
Only her and only him.
Give him a drink, as he asks?

Water, from Jacob's Well,
is life, and life is to share, so,
despite being a woman and Samaritan,
she pours it from the bucket,

drops sparkling in the hot air,
into a cup and gives it to him.
He drinks and drinks and wipes his mouth
and smiles and says, I'll soon be thirsty again.

She smiles in return.
But there is none left,
he says, only Living Water
will keep you eternally refreshed.
Still smiling, still thinking he half jokes,

Give me some of this Living Water, Lord,
she says, for she knows who he is.
He says, Call your husband.

And there, now, she is trapped.
Her past rises up into this sparkling moment.
I have none, she replies.
I know, he says, I know too how many you have had.

And she in return knows him,
for who else would reply so?
A prophet. A Messiah.
So she gives him water for his thirst
and he gives her Life.

All the Other Women

"I read not that ever any man did give unto Christ so much as one groat, but the women followed him and ministered to him of their substance." John Bunyan, Pilgrim's Progress
"Absence from the text is not necessarily absence from the story." Magness, 'Sense'
"…and many others (women) who provided for them out of their means." Luke 8 vs3

Not Counting
Jesus arrives in the next town
and a house is found for the night,
a goat is milked, bread baked,
food picked or bought, washed and cooked,
served.

A sandal is mended, dusty or not,

a sleeve re-sewn, a hem darned,
a headscarf washed, a bed fresh made,
fires lit, comfort assured.

Ordinary healing occurs;
headaches soothed,
toothaches numbed,
fevers reduced,
aching feet washed.

And all the admin:
communication,
messengers found and paid,
organisation of supplies
here and the next town,
connections used,
fundraising for food and travel,
supply lines confirmed.

Invisible, inaudible,
essential, remarkable,
wholehearted cornerstones,
rich in unseen wisdom,
founts of compassion,
buried in two thousand years of dust
and forgetting.
We see you. We salute you. We love you.

Annunciation

A magpie squawks alarm.

From a blue sky a white sun
filigrees the birch tree,
and its leaves
Midas-touch the earth.

They catch.
Gold and bronze
run along dead veins
and dry branches glow deep.
Red glitters up through the air.
Prophecy shimmers in the heat.

Clouds move in.
The fire is snuffed
into a dusty pile.
The magpie takes off,
loose-limbed.

The tree remains,
bare breasted.

*Local artist, Susan Birth, created a painting 'Face the Day' in response to
'Annunciation', it was due to be shown in the Cathedral but could not be
displayed due to lockdown. It can be viewed on Susan Birth's website:*
https://susanbirth.com/

Lent 2021

Lent is here and it's very different to last year. None of my poems is going up on the Cathedral Facebook (they had their outing last year) so I feel a bit lost. However, there are daily services, weekly talks and so many other things on the Cathedral FB. It has exploded over the year. Long may it continue! Especially when we open up, so that those unable to get to services in person can still experience them and feel part of the community. One of the unexpected blessings of the pandemic.

What has been interesting is the series of talks from the Cathedral on the subject of 'Place' during Lent. I started making notes, in order to think about a possible poetic response but it felt like no response was necessary. All that was said was in the talks. Bishop John kicked off introducing the importance and significance of place in the human stories, religious stories i.e., Garden of Eden, travelling from Egypt (a place of suffering) to the Promised Land (a place of safety and belonging). He also drew attention to the holy cities of Jerusalem, Bethlehem, Nazareth, Golgotha, Damascus— real places, with real details and specificity. There is something that takes your breath away when you're in a place where a historically and spiritually significant event took place. I think this is why we visit historical places so much—to make that connection.

One's home is important. Where the hearth is. But if you are a refugee you have to carry the hearth, the heart, with you. Cooking and culture co-exist. There is a danger of 'place idolatry' and being a refugee means forcibly leaving behind significant places and taking with you what is only in your heart and memory. Sacred places also reside within our set of values and priorities and, of course, we can take love anywhere. Canons Michael Brierley, Stephen Edwards and Georgina Byrne gave interesting and sometimes personal talks on Hills, City, and Borders as types of Place, and all show how we adapt and change behaviours and expectations depending on our external surrounding. They are well worth a visit on the virtual 'Place' of the Cathedral Facebook page.

116

So, Lent came to an end, Passiontide arose and moved into Holy Week and then there was Easter. I had a particularly poignant one, thinking of the fact that technically my residence has come to an end. This won't stop me writing about the Cathedral though or being involved in that beautiful building and community.

I want to finish with a poem on ministry. I was cheeky enough to send a questionnaire to the Canons of the Cathedral to find out what motivated them to join the clergy. I am very interested in the concept of vocation, its appeal, its stringencies, its challenges, how it begins, how it's maintained, so I wanted to ask those who had felt, in different ways, that particular call and who heeded it. The questionnaire appears as an Appendix at the end of the book so you can see just how impertinent I really was.

As you will see from the resultant poem, I have not used their answers in direct form. In fact, I cast about for ages for an appropriate metaphor, wracked my brain for fitting images and concepts and then realised that Jesus had got there first and stamped the idea of ministry irrevocably with his inimitable use of simile and parable. So, I gave in and ran with what he had provided first.

Ministry

John 10 vs2

For those who are called,
a shepherd and his flock,
a shepherd and her flock

sounds fetchingly rural,
Gainsborough-like idyllic,
gauzily romantic.

As Gabriel Oak would tell you
it's hedges and fences maintained and checked
at all times, in all weathers,

food and grazing constantly supplied,
nits, lice and worms and worse treated,
foot rot, gut rot and knotted wool too,

lambs delivered throughout days and nights
of snowstorms, rainstorm and
the dark velvet sky of spring stars,

hooked out of reluctant wombs,
slapped into life, cuddled into life,
delivered to mothers, efficient or indifferent.

Shepherds are shepherds all their lives
otherwise sheep get lost, stolen, ill,
stuck, scared, confused, sad, deceived.

So ministry is a question that,
once it is answered by a yes,
is a lifetime of service and love,

a threefold command and a promise,
a schema and a metaphor.
Feed my lambs.
Tend my sheep.
Feed my sheep.

And now I am signing off from the residency. It started out with
very different intentions and plans pre-pandemic, when life was
very different indeed. When in-person events were a possibility and
workshops and poems could be put on display. What has
intervened has been a challenge for all and it has shaped the way my
residency has gone. What it has done for me, personally, has given
me a purpose and a creative vision which I would not have had and
which saw me through the loneliness and difficulties of this plague
year. The Cathedral still stands, still contains the holy silences and
glorious sounds, the dim corners and the brilliant light, and it is
there for all to find and take solace in. I thank the Cathedral and its
Chapter so much for this inimitable experience and hope that these
poems and reflections find favour with them. I look forward to a
continuing relationship in some form.

Thanks

My thanks to Rev Canon Dr Georgina Byrne, Rev Canon Dr Michael Brierley, Rev Canon Dr Stephen Edwards, the Dean, Daniel Parnell, Director of Education, Susan Macleod (Operational Manager), Head Verger James Prior, Vergers Carol Oliver, Nathaniel Hitchings, Undercroft personnel, Song School Director Samuel Hudson, David Morrison, Librarian and Archivist, Polly Stretton, Rod Griffiths and Tony Judge of Black Pear Press, my very supportive family and friends, the wider poetry community including those who contributed to *Call and Response* a poetic anthology (Black Pear Press) that contains different poetic responses to the Cathedral.

Appendix

Ministry/Vocation questions:

1. What was your religious background? Did you come from a practising Christian family?
2. Was asking for ordination in any way a form of rebellion against who/where you were in life?
3. At what point in your life did you know (or even half-know) that ministry was for you? Were you married/single/kids/church member/non-member/other faith member/good place/bad place? or 'other'.
4. Did you recognise the call straight away or was it disguised within something else i.e., a caring occupation such as teaching/nursing/caring/leading etc.
5. Can you describe how it felt? How did it manifest itself (especially if your background wasn't conventionally Christian)—in the body/emotions/outlook?
6. Was it gradual, towards a tipping point? Or was it sudden, even dramatic?
7. What impact has it had on your life a) at the time, b) long term?
8. Best thing about ministry/vocation?
9. Worst thing about ministry/vocation?
10. Do you ever regret your decision?
11. Do you ever doubt your ability to match up to the expectations of being a minister?
12. Did you encounter prejudice regarding your gender/colour on your journey to ordination?

Do you encounter it now? If you didn't encounter prejudice, do you ever reflect on why that is and how to help those who do? Are there any changes you would like to see in the church today re these prejudices? Re any other issues?

Debating Points

Warning! I may be playing Devil's Advocate in some of these questions/statements!

Do you ever think that traditions, paraphernalia, pageantry, costume, theatre etc., can get in the way of (and even negate) attracting some people who may be interested in Jesus' life and message, but do not want 'Churchness'. Can one believe in God and Jesus without being a member of the Church of England?

Are not the basic 'takeaways': trust God, follow Jesus's example, love yourself and others, be kind. These seem to be the minimum requirements, entry-level qualifications if you like, yet how many churchgoers would fail each one? Too simple for our sophisticated palates?

Do we need expensive buildings, statuary, fine books, gold and silver, brocaded vestments, to deliver Jesus' message and follow his example? Are these artefacts not more to do with our cultural heritage rather than any current religious imperative? Still valuable, but in a different category and deserving perhaps of different methods of maintenance.

How difficult (perhaps impossible!) is it to communicate a sense of a personal relationship with God? When/where/how do you experience God? Are there times when you doubt this? How do you get through doubt?

Reviews

Amanda Bonnick's unusual, uplifting and imaginative collection of sixty poems, embedded in a diary covering the period mid-2019 to Easter 2021, is the outcome of her period as Poet in Residence at Worcester Cathedral.

It is a highly personal reflection on her experiences during that time, a 'pilgrimage' as she calls it, and the poems cover both her profound faith, her interviews with the groups making up the Cathedral community—administrators, builders, choristers, clergy and others—and her love for the building itself, 'a place of solace and refuge and beauty'. A reflection on the writing of medieval manuscripts, for example, ends: 'Across the dusty years / his act of grace still glows, / holds the light, / throws back his blessing. / And I, mute, am awestruck…'. A graceful poem about the vergers records their unsung dedication, a poem about bell-ringing displays a teasing array of technical terms, while 'Crypt' begins: 'Can you hear the Cathedral breathing?… This is the sacred engine room / where enlightenment turns, / like a fish in deep waters…' and concludes: 'The breath, the word, / the pneuma, the spirit, / all are one / and all are held here.'

It would be a pleasure to quote many more of Bonnick's rich imagery and insights into Cathedral life, which readers are warmly encouraged to discover for themselves.

As is common current practice, the poems are in free verse, that is, the lines do not rhyme or have a regular pattern of syllables, but there is a strong awareness of rhythm, and occasional use of alliteration and assonance, in other words, a consciousness of the quality and sound of words. Moreover, the emotional content of the poems is often so intense that the form seems immaterial. This applies in particular to two sets of poems which stand apart from the rest, these are the 'Stations of the Cross', the conventional stages of Jesus's last walk to Calvary, and 'Women in the Gospels'. The writer confesses to trepidation at daring to comment on the Biblical account. She need not have worried, for she adds voices that speak cogently to us, today's bystanders at the harrowing event.

The prose diary is very different, although it is sometimes difficult to tell where poetry ends and prose begins. It is a highly personal record, a self-revelation, a confession almost, and those who do not know the writer at the beginning will certainly feel that they know her by the end.

Covid and lockdown make their appearance, and the latter half of the book contains a long dozen pages of lamentation that when the Cathedral closes its doors, 'the sacred breath has contracted to a whisper' and 'my creative cup is empty.' Briefly, she tips over into exaggeration here, saying that 'There are as many examples of suffering as there are people.' But this is born of affection for the Cathedral and what it represents. Ultimately, all the tight-knit poems, and the more expansive diary, are about the power of love in its various forms. As Bonnick says, the conclusion that she draws from her long pilgrimage is: 'Believe the words of love. Ignore the words of power.'

Peter Sutton, poet.

For George MacLeod, founder of the Iona Community after the First World War, a thin place was one where the gap between heaven and earth hardly exists. On that reckoning, Worcester Cathedral has a dizzying store of thinness. In *Solace in the Silence,* Amanda Bonnick gives proper voice to that sacred space: its purpose, its history, its status as a symbol of faith nurtured and sustained—and its power as a refuge from a world that grows more baffling by the hour. 'Careful footsteps pick across intricately inlaid floors,' observes the opening poem; and this serves as a guiding metaphor for the successes and challenges of Amanda's residency— not least the challenge of coronavirus, which, squatting unbudgeably in the middle of the project, necessitated revisions to—even suspensions of—a large part of its schedule.

Solace in the Silence is at once a meditation on faith, an exploration of the Cathedral's architecture (tangible and numinous) and one writer's reflection on her creativity: its flows and roadblocks and, beyond those, its fitness to re-examine narratives and characters long enshrined (and much-recounted) in Christian faith. Concerning this last, two poem-sequences, on the Stations of the Cross and on Women in the Gospels, succeed wonderfully. Familiar stories are reanimated. Women are called out of the shadows to which earlier ecclesiastical hands had casually consigned them. The reader is right alongside Simon of Cyrene as he wrestles with Jesus's cross; they share the confusion of Pilate's wife as she tells herself that this man cannot simply be fodder for the mob's excoriation, that the look in his eyes 'must mean something'.

Surrounding those and the other poems are vivid descriptions of meetings, renovations, and workshops, all set against the different phases of the liturgical year, each phase with its own defined voice. The writer of those descriptions is now hopeful, now uncertain, now perplexed, now transported, emotions which so often inhere in faith itself. From first to last, *Solace in the Silence* invites the reader— believer, non-believer, don't-know—to still themselves and do precisely that.

Michael W. Thomas, writer, poet, playwright, musician.

This experimental collection, which combines memoir and poetry together, creates an atmosphere of meditative adventure, with an observer who possesses a talent for capturing people. The engaging memoir sections are full of drama and thoughtful or wry observations. It becomes journey though the Cathedral, seeking and observing, as well as record of a strange era: lockdown.

The poems give life to stories found in the bible, bringing the human voice to the foreground and giving them a theatrical vividness, as in the poem Joanna, 'I can finally tell you what my life was like.' Amanda Bonnick has created a mesmerising collection that immerses the reader in the Cathedral spaces until heartbeats are heard there amongst the stone walls.

Ruth Stacey, poet and lecturer.

Acknowledgements

'Fifty Years Since Sarawak' *Pick Your Own* (Black Pear Press, 2019)